TRAIN YOUR BRAIN

BRAIN TEASERS TO SHARPEN YOUR MIND

PUZZLER MEDIA LIMITED

SKYHORSE PUBLISHING

Contents

INTRODUCTION

Puzzles are good for your mental health. Research has shown that daily exercises can boost memory and concentration skills. Studies have found a correlation between increased levels of mental stimulation and reduced risk of dementia, while simple acts such as reading aloud, doing arithmetic or solving a puzzle can increase blood flow to the prefrontal cortex, which stimulates activity in the rest of the brain.

Analysis also shows that connections between brain cells can be reinforced by repetition, suggesting that the brain is like a muscle that needs regular stretching.

Here is a collection of daily brain-training exercises to improve the resilience of your mind. Variety, not dificulty, is key so they should prove more fun than maths homework. Enjoy.

Michael Harvey, Features Editor, *The Times*

Workouts
1-190

WORKOUT 1

Wordsearch

TIME

How quickly can you find the five themed words in each grid?

CAKES

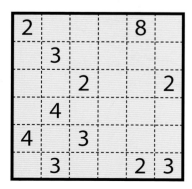

R	I	G	J	L	C	F
R	I	A	L	C	E	V
X	Z	T	S	E	Y	E
N	T	E	P	M	N	Q
D	A	A	B	O	U	H
U	G	U	C	W	B	O
W	K	S	T	A	R	T

FRUIT

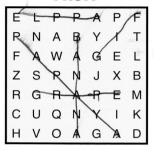

E	L	P	P	A	P	F
R	N	A	B	Y	I	T
F	A	W	A	G	E	L
Z	S	P	N	J	X	B
R	G	R	A	P	E	M
C	U	Q	N	Y	I	K
H	V	O	A	G	A	D

Splits

TIME

Can you rearrange each of these sets of letter blocks into a word?

Discovery

1 RY SCO DI VE   4 TU LO DE NGI

2 RAT TO ED LE   5 ER WH HEV IC

3 OR LIC IT SO   Whichever

Cell Blocks

TIME

2			8	
	3			
		2		2
	4			
4		3		
	3		2	3

Fill the grid by drawing blocks along the gridlines. Each block must be square or rectangular and must contain the number of squares indicated by the digit inside it. Each block must contain only one digit.

8

Sudoku

Place a number in each empty square so that each row, each column and each 2x2 block contains all the numbers from 1-4.

			1
		4	
4	3		
	2		

	3	2	
	1		2
		4	

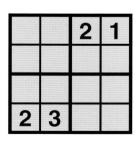

Add Up

If the number in each circle is the sum of the two below it, how quickly can you figure out the top number? Try this one in your head, before writing anything down.

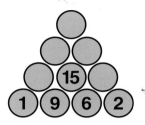

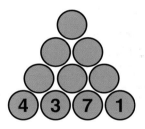

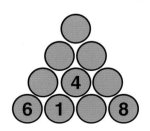

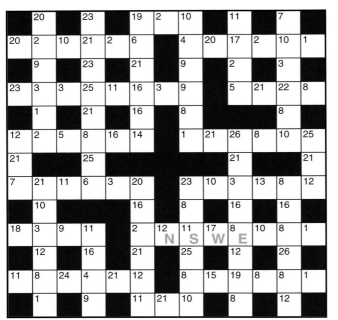

Codeword

TIME

Can you crack the code and fill in the crossword grid? Each letter of the alphabet makes at least one appearance in the grid, and is represented by the same number wherever it appears. The four letters we've decoded should help you to identify other letters and words in the grid.

A B C D **E** F G H I J K L M **N** O P Q R **S** T U V **W** X Y Z

1	2	3	4	5	6	7	8	9	10	11	12	13
							E			**S**	**N**	
14	15	16	17	18	19	20	21	22	23	24	25	26
			W									

Spot the Sum

TIME

In each of these boxes, one of the numbers is the sum of two others. Can you spot the sum?

1

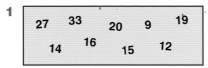

27 33 20 9 19 14 16 15 12

3

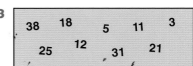

38 18 5 11 3 25 12 31 21

2

10 1 27 7 33 12 21 18 4

4

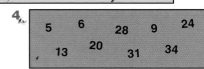

5 6 28 9 24 13 20 31 34

Memory Jog

Spend two minutes memorising this list of twenty words, then see how many of them you can recall on a separate piece of paper in another two minutes.

COURAGE	BLUE	BLITHELY	ANTIQUES
DRILL	SHARPEN	WAGON	MESH
HATSTAND	SITCOM	TEAPOT	PURPOSE
MANNERS	PLASTER	PANTOMIME	SPILL
PARTICULAR	CONTINUE	CELLAR	FORTUNE

Pyramid

Each answer except the first uses all the letters – usually in a different order – from the previous answer plus one extra letter.

1 Personal pronoun I
2 That thing IT
3 Neckwear TIE
4 Row of seats TIER
5 Sluggish TIRED
6 Eye's light-sensitive membrane
7 Piece of ground for military use
8 Hold someone back from action
9 Apprehending

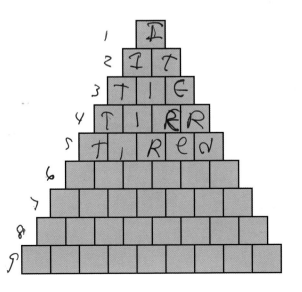

WORKOUT 5

Futoshiki

Fill the blank squares so that each row and column contains all the numbers 1, 2, 3 and 4. Use the given numbers and the symbols that tell you if the number in the square is larger (>) or smaller (<) than the number next to it.

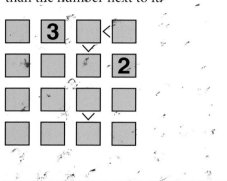

Initials

If ITHOTN (Oscar-winning film) is *IN THE HEAT OF THE NIGHT*, what do these initials represent?

1 WICW (George Formby song)

2 TBM (Nursery rhyme)

3 TLOTR (Film title)

4 TLTWATW (Children's novel)

5 HC (Madonna album)

Shikaku

Divide the Shikaku grid into squares and rectangles, each shape containing a single number that describes exactly how many boxes there are inside it.

			4					
		9						9
					6			
		3		4				
8			4					6
						6		
			3	4			8	
	6	2			4			
				6				2
							6	

12

Fitword

TIME

When all of the listed words have been placed correctly in the grid, which one is left over?

3 letters
Cud
Ego
Emu
Gym
Hit
Jaw
Owe
Sow
Wax
Web

4 letters
Bomb
Defy
Limp
Luck
Nest
Pair
Sawn
Zany

5 letters
Annoy
Aorta
Aroma
Media
Merit
Minus

6 letters
Obtain
Rotund

Six Pack

TIME

Can you place digits in the empty triangles, so that the numbers in each hexagon add up to 25? Only single digits between 1 and 9 can be used, and no two numbers in any hexagon may be the same.

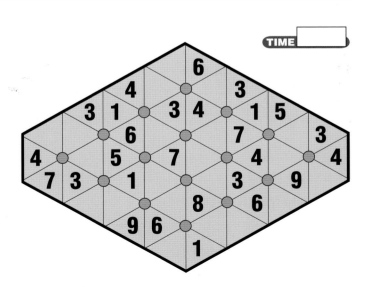

13

WORKOUT 7

Pathfinder

TIME

Beginning with JUDGES, and moving up, down, left or right, one letter at a time, can you trace a path of seventeen Old Testament books?

E	D	L	E	C	I	T	I	V	H	A
U	E	K	I	U	O	N	A	E	L	I
T	Z	E	B	S	J	J	H	R	E	M
E	R	J	O	A	H	O	S	E	J	H
N	O	L	A	B	A	U	H	M	I	A
O	I	E	K	K	J	G	E	S	C	I
M	N	E	K	U	U	D	M	E	A	D
Y	A	X	O	A	H	L	A	N	H	A
N	D	H	D	I	N	A	H	T	O	B
A	H	A	U	S	Z	E	P	A	T	I
M	U	I	M	E	H	E	N	S	N	O

Number Jig

TIME

Which one of the listed numbers won't fit in each of these mini grids?

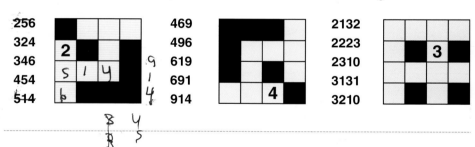

256
324
346
454
514

469
496
619
691
914

2132
2223
2310
3131
3210

Copycats

TIME

Choose the answer that best copies the pattern.

READ is to WRITE as LISTEN is to: Ear • Mime • Look • Speak • Hear

DOG is to KENNEL as SQUIRREL is to: Nest • Holt • Tree • Drey • Hole

JAM is to JAR as TEA is to: Cup • Pot • Caddy • Can • Urn

MILE is to MOLE as MOLE is to: Male • More • Mule • Sole • Mire

Dominoes

 **TIME**

Solve the clues then write the six-letter answers into the dominoes. You must work out whether each word fits in clockwise or anticlockwise, so that the connecting letters of the dominoes all match up.

1 Princess ____, the late Duchess of Kent

2 ____ Eccleston, Formula 1 boss

3 ____ Steptoe, Harold's father

4 Mother ____, Calcutta nun

5 *King* ____, Elvis song and movie

6 ____ Schwarzenegger, film star and Governor of California

Sudoku

 TIME

Use your powers of reasoning to place numbers in the grid, so that each row, each column and each 3x3 block contains the numbers 1-9.

	9	4	3		7	8	2	
2				5				3
3	8						7	4
		7	8		4	5		
	4		2		9		1	
		3				1		
			6	4	5			
	5	2				9	4	

Codewords

 TIME

If HERD is 1234 and ARMY is 5367, how quickly can you work out these collective nouns? You should identify more letters as you go along.

1 8 1 5 3 6

2 8 3 5 9 1

3 9 10 5 3 6

4 6 11 3 4 2 3

5 12 3 13 4 2

WORKOUT 9

Mini Fit

Which one of the listed words won't fit in each of these mini grids?

ACT
APT
CAP
TIP
TIC

DOE
DOR
ORE
RED
ROD

FIVE
FLAT
LAIR
TILE
VIAL

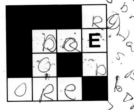

CROW
DOVE
ERNE
ROOK
WREN

Wordsearch

Hidden in this wordsearch grid are eighteen musical instruments.

A	P	T	L	B	A	N	J	O
R	S	E	G	N	O	G	P	N
I	I	N	A	P	M	I	T	A
S	T	I	T	P	C	U	T	I
M	L	R	R	C	B	E	V	R
D	F	A	O	A	P	J	I	E
R	H	L	B	M	L	H	O	O
U	O	C	U	M	B	O	L	B
M	F	R	Y	T	Y	O	I	O
S	T	O	L	L	E	C	N	V
G	U	I	T	A	R	B	G	E

Scramble

What EU capital cities can be made from each of these sets of scrambled letters?

1 MORE *Rome*
2 PAIRS *Paris*
3 HASTEN
4 NO GAP HENCE *Copenhagen*
5 CHERUB SAT
6 PUB DATES
7 MADE SMART
8 STAB A RIVAL

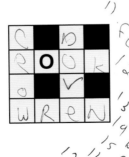

16

Small Change

Can you change one letter of each of these words to make five new words with a common theme?

1   LORD • LOVER • FLAT • SENT • NEXUS

2   HOSE • DAIRY • LILT • IRKS • PALSY

3   FOLD • SALVER • TIC • ICON • LEAF

4   CABLE • CHAIN • DUSK • CREST • PRESSER

Opposites Attract

Can you sort each set of letter blocks into two words with opposite meanings?

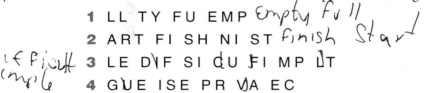

1   LL TY FU EMP   *Empty Full*

2   ART FI SH NI ST   *finish Start*

Difficult Simple   3   LE DF SI du FI MP LT

4   GUE ISE PR VA EC

Vague Precise

Kakuro

Simple addition and a bit of logical thinking will solve this one. You must write a digit in each white square so that the digits in each across section add up to the total in the triangle to the left, and the digits in each column add up to the total in the triangle above. 1-9 are the only digits to use and, although you may find a digit repeated in a row, it must not be repeated in the same section. We've solved one section for you.

WORKOUT 11

Arroword

Just follow the arrows to write your answers in the grid. A handful of anagram clues will get you thinking differently.

CHEEPS (anag) ▼		Thick mist ▼		Sullivan's operetta partner ▼		Small ocean ▼		Makes less strong ▼	Variety of polecat
IMPOSER (anag) ►						▼		Grass road-edging ▼	
Spider's flytrap		Edge of a hat		Go away, depart ►				▼	
►		▼		Decorate (a cake)	BREAK (anag) ►				
Offence, unlawful act ►						Make mistakes ►			
				ANGER (anag) ►					
►						Part of a tennis match ►			
Elegant, stylish	Thaw ►								

Vowel Play

Can you replace the missing vowels to complete the names of these vegetables?

1 C R R T   *Carrot*
2 P T T
3 L T T C   *lettuce*
4 P   *Pea*
5 L K   *leek*
6 K L   *kale*
7 N N   *celery*
8 C L R Y
9 R D S H   *Radish*
10 B T R T

Smart Sums

Try to avoid writing down anything but the final answers to these calculations…

1 Sides on a pentagon x different letters in CABBAGES

2 Squares on a chessboard ÷ quarts in a gallon

3 States in the USA – baker's dozen

4 Consonants in YELLOW + events in a heptathlon

18

Egg-Timer

To answer these clues you have to remove a letter from the previous answer and (if necessary) rearrange the letters to get the new answer. When you pass clue 5, you have to do the opposite – adding a letter each time. We have put in one answer to help you.

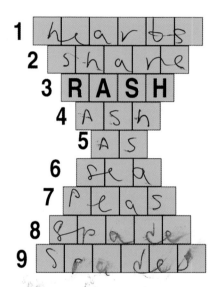

1 hearts
2 share
3 **RASH**
4 ASh
5 AS
6 sea
7 peas
8 spade
9 spades

1 Red suit of cards
2 Divide up among friends
3 ~~Allergy spots~~
4 Powdery fire remains
5 ___ good ___ gold, saying
6 Area of salt water
7 Round green vegetables
8 Digging tool
9 Black suit of cards

Mobile Code

If FEZ is 339 on this phone keypad, which items of headgear have the following numbers?

1 227
2 23738
3 726262
4 874529
5 269537

Four by Four

How quickly can you solve this mini crossword?

¹B	²O	³L	⁴T
⁵A			A
⁶T	A	L	K
⁷S	I	m	E

ACROSS

1 Sliding door-lock
5 Long operatic solo
6 Converse
7 Berry used to flavour gin

DOWN

1 Nocturnal flyers
2 Of the mouth
3 Air bed
4 Extract

WORKOUT 13

Set Square

Place one each of the digits 1-9 in the grid to make the sums work. We've put in some of the numbers to start you off. Sums should be solved from left to right, or from top to bottom.

3 4 5 6 7
8 9

3	+	7	−	2	= 8
−		+		×	
1	+		−	6	= 4
×		÷		+	
5	×	8	−	4	= 12

= 10   = 4   = 20

In and Out

Without changing the order of the letters, add or remove one letter each time to leave a (different) new complete word and put the added or removed letters in their respective boxes to find an accurate small version of a car reading down the boxes.

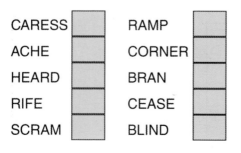

CARESS
ACHE
HEARD
RIFE
SCRAM

RAMP
CORNER
BRAN
CEASE
BLIND

Box Wise

Can you place the three-letter groups in the boxes, so that neighbouring boxes always make a six-letter word, like PAR-DON or DON-ATE? We've placed one group to start you off.

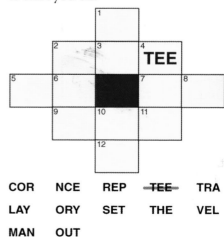

COR	NCE	REP	~~TEE~~	TRA
LAY	ORY	SET	THE	VEL
MAN	OUT			

20

Mini Jigsaw

Fit the pieces in the grid to spell out a type of bird in each row.

TIME

Pieces:
- S E / L E
- G R / O R
- O U / I O
- N N / P R
- C K / O V
- G A / O S
- E T / E Y
- O O / E R
- C U / P L

Grid (rows 1–6):
- Row 2: O
- Row 4: O
- Row 5: O

Killer Sudoku

TIME

The normal rules of Sudoku apply. Place a digit from 1-9 in each empty square so that each row, column and 3x3 block contains all the digits from 1-9. In addition, the digits in each inner shape (marked by dots) must add up to the number in the top corner of that box. No digit can be repeated within an inner shape.

Killer Sudoku grid clues: 18, 7, 12, 4, 3, 1, 29, 9, 18, 12, 17, 13, 12, 6, 20, 3, 17, 7, 3, 16, 11, 21, 15, 15, 14, 8, 3, 7, 19, 9, 15, 8, 16, 13, 8

Staircase

When these agriculture words are correctly fitted in the rows of the grid, another word on the subject will appear down the diagonal staircase.

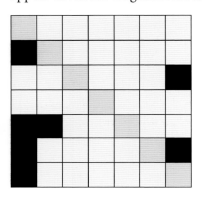

ARABLE	FARMER	YIELD
CROPS	HAYRICK	
DROVERS	PIGLET	

Number Sequence

What number should come next in these sequences?

1 1, 7, 7, 13, 19, 31, ? *4/3 49*

2 3, 3, 5, 4, 4, 3, 5, ? *5 ✓*

3 4, 12, 44, 172, 684, ? *2048 2730*

4 1, 1, 2, 6, 24, 120, 720, ? *5040*

5 1, 4, 13, 40, 121, 364, ? *45 45*

C ×3+)) +093

Word Builder

Using the nine letters provided, can you answer these clues? Every answer must include the highlighted letter T. Which museum in Russia uses all nine letters?

5 Letters
Striped wildcat
Angry
Power
Consumer
Boat Race crew

6 Letters
Amass
Any of two
Profession
Warming appliance
Spat

7 Letters
Type of jazz
More muscular
Arab leader's domain

8 Letters
Move abroad
National history

Wild Words

TIME

What well-known phrases and expressions are suggested by these word pictures?

① **THINK THINK**   **②** RO**THECLOCK**CK

③ 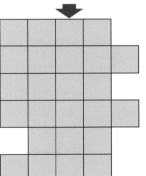   **④** **B E A N**

Fare's Fair

TIME

Find two words of the same sound but different spelling to satisfy each two-element clue, then decide which of the pair goes where in the grid to discover a story in episodes, reading down the arrowed column.

Civic leader's horse

Reported the bells rang

Painful tool

Flower in lines

Hold back money-order

Correct way to put pen to paper

Elimination

TIME

All but two of the listed words fall into one of the four categories. Put these leftover words together, and what phrase do they make?

CATEGORIES Dairy • Words following HAND (e.g., Held) • Gases • Boxing terms

Spar	Whey	Shake	Well	Yogurt	Ropes
Cuff	Neon	Some	Oxygen	Gloves	Brie
Done	Cheese	Argon	Corner	Made	
Set	Ring	Milk	Methane	Hydrogen	

Niners

 TIME

Form four nine-letter words using all twelve listed "syllables" (without altering the order of the letters in each "syllable"). Then enter them in the grid in the right order to reveal a small branch reading down the left-hand column.

ANT	DOL	ESC
GON	IDE	IER
INE	LDW	LEG
OPE	TEL	WOR

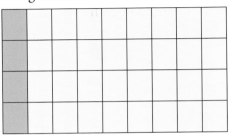

Memory Jog

Spend two minutes memorising this list of twenty words, then see how many of them you can recall on a separate piece of paper.

MEANDER	CHORTLE	CLING	SLAT	EXTRA
CUMMER-BUND	WHIM	BILL	BUBBLE	BENCH
STAMP	EERILY	BESIDE	ARROW	
CERTAINLY	CLOWN	FESTIVAL	JUSTLY	
	MAGPIE	MELTING		

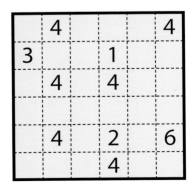

Cell Blocks

 TIME

Fill the grid by drawing blocks along the gridlines. Each block must be square or rectangular and must contain the number of squares indicated by the digit inside it. Each block must contain only one digit.

Sudoku

Place a number in each empty square so that each row, each column and each 2x2 block contains all the numbers from 1-4.

	2	3	
3			2
1			3
	3	1	

2			4
	4	2	
	1	4	
4			1

	2	3	
3			2
2			4
	4	2	

Add Up

If the number in each circle is the sum of the two below it, how quickly can you figure out the top number? Try this one in your head, before writing anything down.

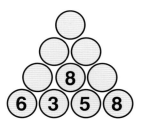

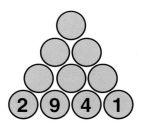

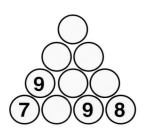

WORKOUT 19

TIME _____

Codeword

Can you crack the code and fill in the crossword grid? Each letter of the alphabet makes at least one appearance in the grid, and is represented by the same number wherever it appears. The four letters we've decoded should help you to identify other letters and words in the grid.

26	19	7	12		22	7	19	14	8	17	11
8		2		15		19		8		8	
18	8	16	12	19	21	9		13	8	17	25	21
25		24		17		2		25		12		25
	16	3	21	2	22	7	25		15	20	19	14
2 **A**		25		12			17		3			19
15 **S**	12	21	25	2	5		10	8	23	23	25	21
12 **T**		11		8			17		2			10
3 **U**	17	10	19		4	2	17	10	25	21	15
12		21		15		15		19		16		8
25	1	2	7	12		15	7	19	15	20	25	10
		23		9		25		21		25		7
	11	2	6	25	12	12	25		25	10	11	9

~~A~~ B C D E F G H I J K L M N O P Q R ~~S~~ ~~T~~ ~~U~~ V W X Y Z

1	2	3	4	5	6	7	8	9	10	11	12	13
	A	**U**									**T**	
14	15	16	17	18	19	20	21	22	23	24	25	26
	S											

Copycats

TIME _____

Choose the answer that best copies the pattern.

TEAPOT is to POUR as KEY is to: Skeleton • Ring • Door • Open • Fob

UMBRELLA is to RAIN as PARASOL is to: Beach • Water • Sun • Cloud • Shade

DABC is to ABCD as SPQR is to: QPRS • SRPQ • RPQS • PQRS • QRSP

PILOT is to FLY as CHAUFFEUR is to: Sail • Drive • Steer • Car • Limousine

POET is to TOPE as PAST is to: Taps • Mind • Spat • Pats • Asps

Splits

Can you rearrange each of these sets of letter blocks into a word?

1 TE EFS BE AK
2 LI ED MIT UN
3 ANT RE ND DU

4 GN URE AT SI
5 ER GO OTH DM

Shape Up

Can you arrange these five-letter shapes into their correct positions in the grid so that ten artists read down the columns?

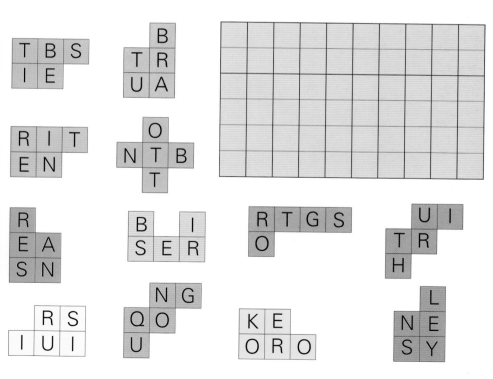

27

Futoshiki

Fill the blank squares so that each row and column contains all the numbers 1, 2, 3, and 4. Use the given numbers and the symbols that tell you if the number in the square is larger (>) or smaller (<) than the number next to it.

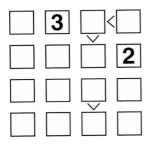

Scramble

What items of footwear can be made from each of these sets of scrambled letters?

1 HOSE

5 BUG ROE

2 TAPS

6 RIPPLES

3 TAKES

7 ALLIED REPS

4 TRIAGE

8 LINNET GLOW

Pet Talk

Which numbered photo has been taken?

28

Fitword

When all of the listed words have been placed correctly in the grid, which one is left over?

TIME

4 letters
Alms
Drat
Holt
Imam
Mall
Ugly

5 letters
Agile
Kitty
Scout
Shade
Stoke

6 letters
Costly
Creamy

7 letters
Acronym
~~Immoral~~

9 letters
Cascading
Disembark

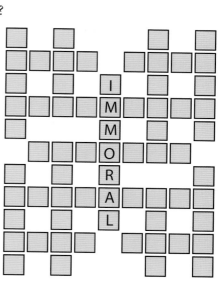

Mind the Gap

TIME

Can you place a well-known three-letter word in the spaces of each row to complete the seven-letter word? Do it correctly, and the shaded letters should spell out an African creature.

T	E				U	S
A				E	M	Y
A	C				A	T
A				A	N	T
F	O	R				R
I	N	S				D
A	F				M	S
A	W	A				G

Pathfinder

TIME

Beginning with PIRATE SHIP, and moving up, down, left or right, one letter at a time, can you trace a path of seventeen types of boat?

P	A	T	H	I	S	H	I	P	B	A
I	R	E	S	P	E	L	G	E	G	R
F	F	I	R	T	T	A	L	L	L	E
C	S	K	I	B	A	C	Y	R	R	O
O	N	A	M	E	U	A	T	F	E	N
R	A	R	O	U	Q	I	A	O	H	D
A	A	T	H	S	E	B	O	W	R	B
C	O	B	W	N	P	R	E	M	O	O
L	E	P	O	A	O	S	P	O	T	A
V	I	R	R	R	O	L	P	A	C	T
A	T	E	E	R	C	L	I	N	O	E

Soundalikes

TIME

Can you complete each of these sentences with two words that sound alike, but are spelt differently?

1. Little Jimmy ___ the ball ___ the hoop.
2. ___ Fido cut his ___ on some glass in the park.
3. '___ can I ~~wear~~ my new shoes?' she cried.
   where

Honeycomb

TIME

Write the six-letter answers clockwise round their respective cell-numbers, starting at the arrowed cell. On completion, you will find that the unclued answers (10 and 11) will reveal the author of *Nineteen Eighty-four*.

1 University award
2 Servant performing menial tasks
3 Look out!
4 *The Origin of Species* author
5 He shrinks from danger
6 Folk
7 Preaching "box" in a church
8 Picnic basket
9 Sawn timber

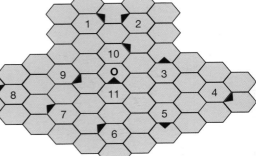

Set Square

TIME

Place one each of the digits 1-9 in the grid to make the sums work. We've put in some of the numbers to start you off. Sums should be solved from left to right, or from top to bottom.

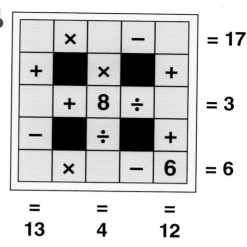

Sudoku

TIME

Use your powers of reasoning to place numbers in the grid, so that each row, each column and each 3x3 block contains the numbers 1-9.

					4	5		
6			7	8			1	
5			6					4
	5	9		7				
	8	7		3		2	5	
				9		4	7	
7					9			6
	3			6	7			8
		8	3					

Initials

TIME

If ITHOTN (Oscar-winning film) is *IN THE HEAT OF THE NIGHT*, what do these initials represent?

1 AFINIAFI (Proverb)

2 TOCS (Dickens novel)

3 HFB (*Fawlty Towers* catchphrase)

4 OFOTCN (Jack Nicholson film)

5 BABP (Dessert)

Fix Six TIME

The six authors listed will fit into this pattern of six adjoining hexagons. All are entered clockwise from a triangle to be discovered. Adjoining triangles always contain the same letter. The P and T give you a start.

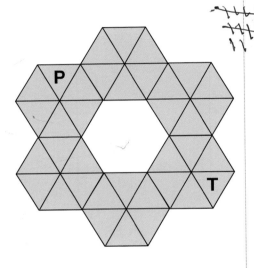

BRONTË   O'BRIEN

DEXTER   RANKIN

JEROME   UPDIKE

Wordsearch TIME

Hidden in this wordsearch grid are fifteen Winnie the Pooh words.

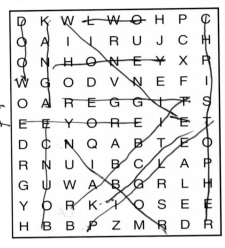

Picture Pair TIME

Which two pictures are identical?

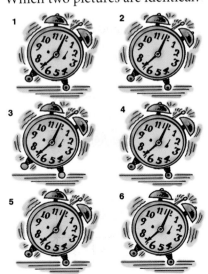

Number Jig

Which one of the listed numbers won't fit in each of these mini grids?

234
372
439
749
792

158
165
567
815
826

1725
3129
5371
6212
7239

Small Change

Can you change one letter of each of these words to make five new words with a common theme?

1 SCORE • PART • FUN • CARE • PIT

2 TURN • LACE • FOOL • FOND • MORE

3 STORE • ROUND • DON • GRIM • DUNCE

4 SHORES • SKINT • KILO • MOWN • PRESS

Kakuro

Simple addition and a bit of logical thinking will solve this one. You must write a digit in each white square so that the digits in each across section add up to the total in the triangle to the left, and the digits in each column add up to the total in the triangle above. 1-9 are the only digits to use and, although you may find a digit repeated in a row, it must not be repeated in the same section. We've solved one section for you.

WORKOUT 27

Arroword

Just follow the arrows to write your answers in the grid. A handful of anagram clues will get you thinking differently.

Convince or guarantee ▼	Pig's enclosure	▼	Projecting rock	▼	ELM (anag)	▼	Hand-held percussion instruments	Sumptuous meal
Easy-to-peel citrus fruit ►				▼			LIMES (anag)	
Stick (out)	Gossip		RESET (anag) ►				▼	
►		▼	Colour (hair)	Vice ►				
Aircraft location system ►		▼			US spy organisation (inits) ►			
►			Ellipses ►					
Depend (on)	Large brown seaweed ►				Full collection ►			

Take Five

The three answers in this mini-crossword read the same across and down. We've clued the three answers, but not in the right order. See how quickly you can solve it.

Permit

The shinbone

Commonplace, trite

Two of a Kind

Can you sort each set of letter blocks into two words with the same meaning?

1 CE PR ER DE NT OP

2 CE AL ECI SP OI CH

3 TA KER NIT OR RE JA CA

4 OT NT PI SP OI NP

5 TAN TU ON RO EO IMP SP US MP

34

Wordsearch

How quickly can you find the five themed words in each grid?

RAIN

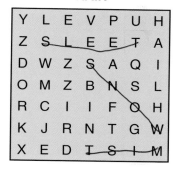

SHOWER

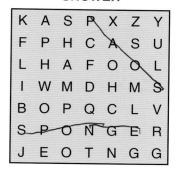

SHINE

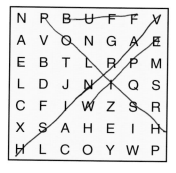

Vowel Play

Can you replace the missing vowels to complete these one-word TV shows?

Doctors

1 DCTRS   **6** CSLTY

2 SPKS   **7** MRS

3 CST   **8** LST

4 HSTL   **9** PNRM

5 NWSNGHT   **10** CNTDWN

Countdown

Three in One

The three parts of each clue lead to the same answer word. Can you solve any before you reach the third part?

1 Scratch • Film music • Twenty

2 Carry • Suffer • Ursine creature

3 Song • Set (down) • Non-clergy

4 Golf stroke • Ambition
   • Take the wheel

5 Chute • Hair clip • Slip

Missing Link

The three words in each clue have a fourth word in common, and that's your answer. For example, the clue "Moon • Navy • Royal" gives the answer BLUE (blue moon, navy blue, royal blue). Write each answer in the grid, and the shaded column will reveal a game.

1 Awake • Eyed • Open

2 Dog • Fish • Turn

3 Child • Intensive • Worn

4 Bun • Chair • Salts

5 Acid • Drive • Tube

Codewords

If FLAG=1234 and IRON=5678, how quickly can you work out these golf words? You should identify more letters as you go along.

1 9 3 4 2 9

2 10 7 2 9

3 11 3 2 2

4 11 5 6 12 5 9

5 13 7 7 12

6 13 9 12 4 9

Mind the Gap

Can you complete the five words in each set by adding the same three-letter word? For example OUR in HLY, VIG, FTH (hourly, vigor, fourth), and so on.

1 IMUS PARA PITE CARED CRUMS

2 ADD BEF FLT FST MISH

3 LER FISH SLE POCK GLEN

4 RED GUS DECT PERCTORY PRODITY

5 ITAL PROY CARAN INENT PEREE

Mini Jigsaw

Fit the pieces in the grid to spell out a colour in each row.

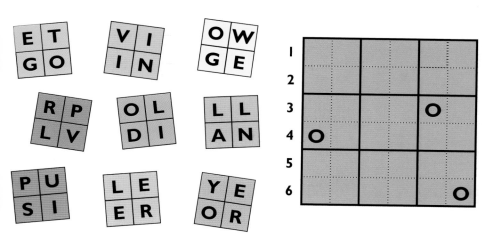

Killer Sudoku

TIME

The normal rules of Sudoku apply. Place a digit from 1-9 in each empty square so that each row, column and 3x3 block contains all the digits from 1-9. In addition, the digits in each inner shape (marked by dots) must add up to the number in the top corner of that box. No digit can be repeated within an inner shape.

WORKOUT 31

Mini Fit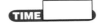

Which one of the listed words won't fit in each of these mini grids?

HIT
OPT
THY
TIP
TOY

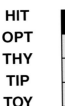

IMP
MAT
SAW
SUM
TWO

BELT
BOTH
LATE
TUBE
TUTU

DARE
DEAF
DENT
FAIR
FRET

Word Builder

Using the nine letters provided, can you answer these clues? Every answer must include the highlighted letter C. What source of music uses all nine letters?

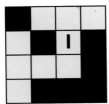

5 Letters
Instruct _teach_
Frighten _scare_
Tedious job
Crate
Bedlam
Pursue

6 Letters
Look (for) _search_
Thespians _actors_
Type of sugar _~~sucrose~~_
Bodice

7 Letters
More vulgar _harsher_
Portable lights
Drinks mat _coaster_
Toxophilites

8 Letters
Makers
Energy-releasing devices

Splits

TIME

Can you rearrange each of these sets of letter blocks into a word? (As a bonus, you should spot a link between each word once correctly rearranged. What is the link?)

Porcupine

1 NE POR PI CU

Companion

4 ION AN MP CO

2 DI NE ST SHO

5 UG ERS GL SM

3 ATE OK BO PL

Smugglers

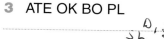

Dist shone

Memory Jog

You have two minutes to study the list of twenty words. Then give yourself another two minutes to write as many as you can recall on a separate piece of paper.

COLOR	DOWNPOUR	FAN	OPENLY
BLANK	AFFABLE	POSTCARD	SPREAD
SPINE	WONDERMENT	FORK	COSTUME
COLLECT	ENVELOPE	CABLE	VOCAL
SPEEDILY	SHOWER	HOARSE	STICK

Pairs

TIME

Pair off 24 of the listed words to form twelve "double-barreled" words and rearrange the letters of the two words left over to reveal a fruit.

BANK	DIVING	OPENER
BISCUIT	FIRE	PONY
BOARD	HOLIDAY	RACKET
BOTTLE	INSURANCE	SKIN
CAMP	LACE	SQUASH
CHEESE	LEANT	STOP
CLAIM	LEMON	TAIL
COCK	MOWER	TEA
CUP	NECK	

Wordsearch

How quickly can you find the five themed words in each grid?

SPORTS

C	X	V	G	B	M	A
S	Y	E	K	C	O	H
I	U	C	Q	O	L	C
N	O	H	L	D	T	N
N	E	O	J	I	Z	Y
E	P	W	R	S	N	F
T	K	G	O	L	F	G

HERBS

B	O	L	L	I	D	T
H	R	M	X	L	H	V
F	E	L	I	Y	M	I
P	G	S	M	N	C	D
G	A	E	A	U	T	Z
B	N	J	N	E	T	K
R	O	Q	W	O	S	Y

Set Square

Place one each of the digits 1-9 in the grid to make the sums work. We've put in some of the numbers to start you off. Sums should be solved from left to right, or from top to bottom.

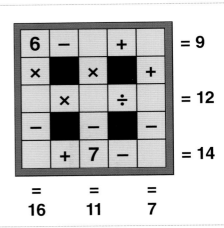

Cell Blocks

Fill the grid by drawing blocks along the gridlines. Each block must be square or rectangular and must contain the number of squares indicated by the digit inside it. Each block must contain only one digit.

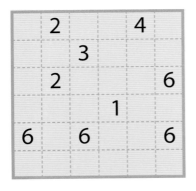

Sudoku

Place a number in each empty square so that each row, each column and each 2x2 block contains all the numbers from 1-4.

1			4
	4	1	
	1	3	
3			1

	1	3	
3			1
2			3
	3	2	

3			4
	4	3	
	2	4	
4			2

Add Up

If the number in each circle is the sum of the two below it, how quickly can you figure out the top number? Try this one in your head, before writing anything down.

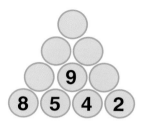

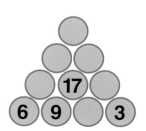

41

20	25	8	9	12	8	8	9		8	1	1	4
15		25		22		23		6		8		20
15	6	20	9	1		12	18	11	26	3	22	1
8		24		8		22		24		11		8
9	11	8	1		20	13	9	8		13	8	3
	12			15		23		14		8		
5	8	17	24	3	8		17	20	23	1	20	9
	3		26		22		19			16		
21	9	20	2	22	2 (M)	8		10	26	23	4	
11		11		22		21 (P)		5		2		22
21	8	7	11	23	22	26 (A)		26	2	14	3	8
22		8		13		3 (L)		3		8		3
3	26	1	4		3	26	14	20	11	9	8	1

A B C D E F G H I J K L̸ M̸ N O P̸ Q R S T U V W X Y Z

1	2 M	3 L	4	5	6	7	8	9	10	11	12	13
14	15	16	17	18	19	20	21 P	22	23	24	25	26 A

Codeword

Can you crack the code and fill in the crossword grid? Each letter of the alphabet makes at least one appearance in the grid, and is represented by the same number wherever it appears. The four letters we've decoded should help you to identify other letters and words in the grid.

So Complete

Complete each trio of words with a common letter. The five letters will form the answer word. Where there is a choice of completing letter, you must decide which is needed.

SA_E	GOL_	LI_T	
PA_N	P_ER	CH_P	
WA_E	_EAR	RIN_	
AC_E	C_EF	_EAL	
S_EM	HAL_	FIS_	

Splits

Can you rearrange each of these sets of letter blocks into a word?

1 HO PL USE AY

2 DE CO NT NFI

3 PE NG RI SHI

4 IND RE MA ER

5 ES TT LE OME

Pieceword

With the help of the Across clues only, can you fit the 16 pieces into their correct positions in the empty grid (which, when completed, will exhibit a symmetrical pattern)?

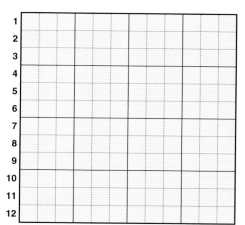

ACROSS

1 Twisted, warped

2 Popular myth

3 Substitute

4 Movie theater

5 Dampening

6 Animal that suckles its young

7 *Away in a ___*, carol

8 High singing voice

9 To an excessive degree

10 Frosty atmosphere

11 Surround, put in a box

12 Slum district

Letter Sequence

TIME

What letter should replace the question mark in these sequences?

1 A, E, J, P, W, E, ?

2 L, I, J, F, G, B, ?

3 M, Q, M, I, M, U, M, E, ?

4 A, L, C, N, E, P, G, R, ?

5 Z, Y, W, T, P, K, ?

Mobile Code

TIME

If EXETER is 393837 on this phone keypad, what other British cities have the following numbers?

1 2284

2 4855

3 9675

4 53337

5 386333

6 2273433

Disavowel

TIME

Can you complete this puzzle by adding all the vowels? There are 13 As, 15 Es, 3 Is, 7 Os and 5 Us in the puzzle.

		R		P			N	■	P	■
	R		M		■	F		R		M
S	N			L	■	F	R		M	
	■	S	T			R	■	T		R
L		T	■	T	R		D		■	C
■	N	■	S	T		Y	■	D		Y
S		R			S	■		■		■
■	R		N	■		N	D		R	
C		N	K		R	■	D	R		W
		T	■	L	■	B		G	■	
	S	S		F	Y	■	R			R

Fitword

When all of the listed words have been placed correctly
in the grid, which one is left over?

TIME

4 letters

Dull

Echo

~~Eden~~

Mull

Note

Opus

Play

Semi

Shun

Tint

Urge

6 letters

Losing

Niggle

Tested

Traced

9 letters

Podginess

Scripting

E D E N

Smart Sums

TIME

Try to avoid writing down anything but the final answers to
these calculations... no counting on fingers allowed either!

1   Legs on a tripod x hours in two-and-a-half days

2   Hearts in a pack of cards + 'S's in POSSESSES

3   Syllables in CORIANDER x lives of a cat

4   Degrees in a circle ÷ consonants in WONDERFUL

5   Stripes on the US flag – number of Olympic rings

Pathfinder

Beginning with MARTIN,
and moving up, down, left or right,
one letter at a time, can you trace a
path of nineteen Saints?

L	E	A	D	M	T	I	N	D	A	L
D	I	N	A	A	R	E	B	R	X	E
A	V	E	S	T	E	R	N	A	A	N
D	I	R	E	H	B	A	Z	I	L	D
P	E	T	H	L	U	C	A	S	E	E
F	R	E	T	O	J	Y	M	A	P	R
R	A	E	W	S	E	H	O	U	O	U
C	N	M	O	L	P	T	E	L	L	I
I	R	T	H	O	H	H	N	I	D	S
S	A	B	N	E	L	E	N	C	E	B
G	A	B	R	I	E	L	A	T	N	E

Box Wise

Can you place the three-letter groups
in the boxes, so that neighboring
boxes always make a six-letter word,
like PAR-DON or DON-ATE? We've
placed one group to start you off.

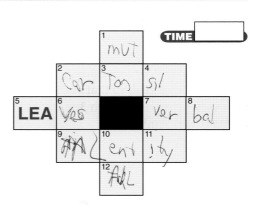

AIL   ENT   MUT   TON

BAL   ITY   SIL   VER

CAR   LEA   TAL   VES

Logical

Three horse-racing brothers won the top three places in the most recent
Grand Multinational steeplechase. From the information given, can you say
which brother rode which horse and in what position they finished?

**If Brendan wasn't the brother who rode Red Rose to victory,
and if Connor on Desert Dahlia finished immediately behind
Aldan, who rode Lilac Lilac and where did they finish?**

Set Square

TIME

Place one each of the digits 1-9 in the grid to make the sums work. We've put in some of the numbers to start you off. Sums should be solved from left to right, or from top to bottom.

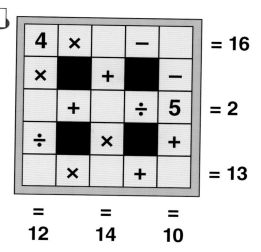

Sudoku

TIME

Use your powers of reasoning to place numbers in the grid, so that each row, each column and each 3x3 block contains the numbers 1-9.

	6	4						
9			6					1
3		5	2			9		7
	7	2		5		1		
			8		3			
			1		5			8
		6	4		8		9	2
						3	1	
	4	3			7	8		

Staircase

TIME

When the seven Scottish clans are correctly placed along the horizontal rows, the letters in the diagonal "staircase" will yield an eighth.

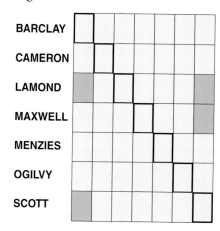

BARCLAY

CAMERON

LAMOND

MAXWELL

MENZIES

OGILVY

SCOTT

Mini Fit

Which one of the listed words won't fit in each of these mini grids?

ANT
APE
MAT
NET
PET

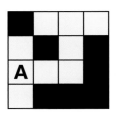

PAL
PIP
PLY
PRY
RIP

 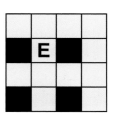

BALL
LEAP
PLOT
TAPE
TELL

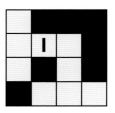

BABY
BANK
BLOB
BLUR
NEON

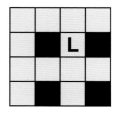

Wordsearch

Hidden in this wordsearch grid are fifteen words that follow red.

L	K	L	R	T	F	L	A	G
Q	A	E	V	L	N	C	X	D
H	E	R	R	I	N	G	E	L
A	F	R	I	W	E	D	Y	I
W	N	I	C	M	N	P	E	G
P	B	U	G	A	D	Y	A	H
S	T	Q	H	U	R	A	H	T
S	A	S	J	L	H	P	M	S
D	E	D	O	O	L	B	E	P
G	M	A	T	D	Z	O	A	T
R	E	P	P	E	P	C	E	I

Scramble

What dogs can be made from each of these sets of scrambled letters?

1 ROB EX

2 EEL BAG

3 LOOPED

4 PROTEIN

5 WITH PEP

6 HER CURL

7 ANT ALIAS

8 SEEK PINE

Niners

Form four nine-letter words using all twelve listed "syllables" (without altering the order of the letters in each "syllable"). Then enter them in the grid in the right order to reveal daybreak reading down the left-hand column.

AND	ARC	COU
DIS	ECT	HIT
HST	IAN	NOR
RSE	WEG	WIT

Memory Jog

Spend two minutes memorising this list of twenty words, then see how many of them you can recall on a separate piece of paper in another two minutes.

COW	TASTE	MESSAGE	ANGRY	PAPER
SKEWER	KEYS	YELLOW	FROG	PIANO
CANDLE	SEVEN	FIZZ	PEACH	SPOON
FINGER	TALK	SHINE	CHAIR	PEANUT

Kakuro

Simple addition and a bit of logical thinking will solve this one. You must write a digit in each white square so that the digits in each across section add up to the total in the triangle to the left, and the digits in each column add up to the total in the triangle above. 1-9 are the only digits to use and, although you may find a digit repeated in a row, it must not be repeated in the same section. We've solved one section for you.

Arroword

TIME

Just follow the arrows to write your answers in the grid. A handful of anagram clues will get you thinking differently.

Genuine ▼		Go backwards ▼		Large monkey ▼		Mad with worry ▼		Word of farewell ▼
►								
Ecological political group (5,5)		Chimney deposit		RITE (anag)		__ Kourni-kova, tennis player		Consume (medicine)
►		▼		▼ TAN (anag) ►		▼		▼ Went in front
STEER (anag)	From the East ►							▼
►				Greek goddess of victory ►				
Hangman's loop	Resembling a series of steps ►							

Initials

TIME

If ITHOTN (Oscar-winning film) is *IN THE HEAT OF THE NIGHT*, what do these initials represent?

1 KOTG (Park notice)

2 JATB (Pantomime)

3 MHMLW (Proverb)

4 TPOTO (Musical)

5 BCATSK (Western)

Number Sequence

TIME

What number should come next in these sequences?

1 1, 2, 5, 10, 17, ?

2 100, 90, 81, 73, 66, ?

3 5, 10, 9, 18, 17, ?

4 1, 2, 5, 14, 41, ?

5 1, 2, 5, 10, 20, 50, ?

Dominoes

Solve the clues then write the six-letter answers into the dominoes. You must work out whether each word fits in clockwise or anticlockwise, so that the connecting letters of the dominoes all match up.

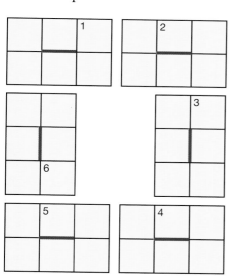

1 ___ Bear, cartoon bear from Nutwood
2 ___ Daley, George Cole's character in *Minder*
3 ___ *the Tank Engine*
4 *Shameless* actress, ___ Peake
5 ___ Woodward, wife of Paul Newman
6 ___ of Arimathea, biblical character

Mobile Code

If RED is 733 on this phone keypad, what colours have the following numbers?

1 2583
2 4653
3 7465
4 47336
5 787753

Four by Four

How quickly can you solve this mini crossword?

ACROSS
1 Prepare food
5 Fairy tale's second word?
6 Throw off track
7 Run away

DOWN
1 End of a sleeve
2 Milk-white gem
3 Seep out
4 Joint in the leg

Fare's Fair

Find two words of the same sound but different spelling to satisfy each two-element clue, then decide which of the pair goes where in the grid to discover a clergyman or chess piece, reading down the arrowed column.

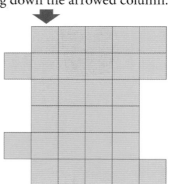

Young swan's ring

Flatfish's position

Fragrance dispatched

Purchaser of cattle-shed

Occasion for herb

Grieve early in the day

Futoshiki

Fill the blank squares so that each row and column contains all the numbers 1, 2 and 3. Use the given numbers and the symbols that tell you if the number in the square is larger (>) or smaller (<) than the number next to it.

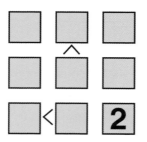

Staircase

When the seven foods are correctly placed along the horizontal rows, the letters in the diagonal "staircase" will yield an eighth.

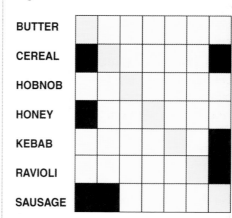

BUTTER

CEREAL

HOBNOB

HONEY

KEBAB

RAVIOLI

SAUSAGE

Mini Jigsaw

Fit the pieces in the grid to spell out a vegetable in each row.

N	N
L	E

T	O
O	W

P	O
M	A

I	P
O	T

F	E
C	E

R	N
R	R

E	L
R	Y

T	U
C	A

T	A
R	R

		E			
1					
2					R
3		T			
4					
5					
6					T

Killer Sudoku

The normal rules of Sudoku apply. Place a digit from 1-9 in each empty square so that each row, column and 3x3 block contains all the digits from 1-9. In addition, the digits in each inner shape (marked by dots) must add up to the number in the top corner of that box. No digit can be repeated within an inner shape.

Cages: 17, 11, 23, 15, 7, 7, 6, 24, 14, 12, 8, 6, 3, 7, 23, 12, 19, 20, 11, 13, 9, 9, 11, 11, 17, 16, 4, 14, 3, 12, 7, 15, 19

Sudoku TIME

Place a number in each empty square so that each row, each column and each 2x2 block contains all the numbers from 1-4.

	1	2	
4			3
	3	4	
1			2

	1		
4		2	
	2		3
		1	

	1		2
	4		3
	2		1
	3		4

Word Builder TIME

Using the nine letters provided, can you answer these clues? Every answer must include the highlighted letter C. What authority figure uses all nine letters?

P	E	A
O	C	L
N	I	M

5 Letters
Kayak
Desert animal
Contagious fear
Ground-up beef
Spotless
Edible nut

6 Letters
Sketching tool
Popular edible fish
Picture house
Wages

7 Letters
Positioned correctly (2,5)
Big-billed bird

8 Letters
Grumble

Alpha-Fit

Each of the 26 letters of the alphabet appears once in this crossword.

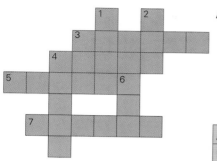

ACROSS
3 Changing residence (6)
5 Sounds like a duck (6)
7 Soft, gentle breeze (6)

DOWN
1 People (4)
2 Three-cornered sail (3)
4 Polished (5)
6 Pig's enclosure (3)

A	B	C	D	E	F	G	H	I	J	K	L	M
N	O	P	Q	R	S	T	U	V	W	X	Y	Z

Six Pack

Can you place digits in the empty triangles, so that the numbers in each hexagon add up to 25? Only single digits between 1 and 9 can be used, and no two digits in any hexagon may be the same.

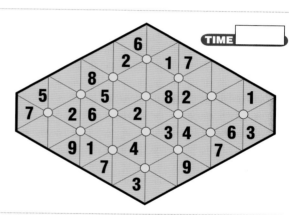

Spot the Sum

In each of these boxes, one of the numbers is the sum of two others. Can you spot the sum?

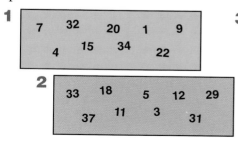

1
7 32 20 1 9
4 15 34 22

2
33 18 5 12 29
37 11 3 31

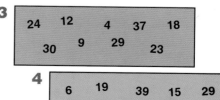

3
24 12 4 37 18
30 9 29 23

4
6 19 39 15 29
8 35 26 30

55

WORKOUT 49

Elimination

All but two of the listed words fall into one of the four categories.
Put these leftover words together, and what phrase do they make?

CATEGORIES Musical instruments • Words preceding PIECE (e.g., Two) • Words without vowels • Reptiles

Myrrh	Square	Conversation	Turtle	Lynx	Master
Anaconda	Triangle	Bassoon	Meal	Viola	Iguana
Cymbals	Why	Crypt	Party	Hair	
Time	Cobra	Cornet	Alligator	Rhythm	

Logical

How quickly can you figure out what's what?

Implausible though it seems, three students have a rota of household chores for Monday, Tuesday and Wednesday. If Andrew's task is on Tuesday, but is not the ironing, and the dusting is carried out later in the week than Brian's gardening, what does Colin do and on which day?

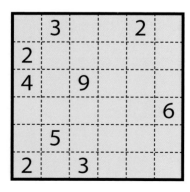

Cell Blocks

Fill the grid by drawing blocks along the gridlines. Each block must be square or rectangular and must contain the number of squares indicated by the digit inside it. Each block must contain only one digit.

Wordsearch

How quickly can you find the five themed words in each grid?

BREAKFAST

T	G	I	E	S	H	N
F	R	L	E	G	Q	O
Y	B	S	I	V	G	C
M	C	E	J	D	P	A
T	R	U	G	O	Y	B
N	K	M	W	Z	A	L
T	O	A	S	T	U	O

ANIMAL NOISES

W	Y	E	B	U	D	G
T	F	N	P	A	O	O
Z	O	Y	N	B	A	C
R	O	H	B	I	A	V
F	W	L	I	G	H	X
Q	E	S	J	N	M	W
Q	U	A	C	K	K	B

WATER ___

G	T	P	R	O	O	F
N	I	X	K	F	L	M
J	U	B	L	O	A	A
O	C	W	T	R	F	E
P	S	S	K	V	F	C
Q	I	H	U	D	U	Z
P	B	S	M	T	B	R

Add Up

If the number in each circle is the sum of the two below it, how quickly can you figure out the top number? Try this one in your head, before writing anything down.

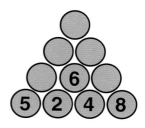

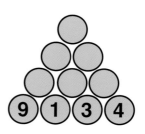

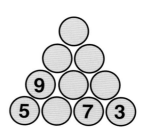

WORKOUT 51

	26	2	8	9	12	20	20		20	14	6	3
11		1		6		16		23		2		12
19	12	12	17	8		2	22	15	6	7	10	6
23			12		1		25		18			13
20	24	25	6	22	12	1		6	15	2	15	
11		5			8		7		22			19
12	5	11	12	7	1		19	6	22	21	11	16
1		22		12		3		2				12
	7	2	4	6		2	25	11 (T)	1 (D)	2 (O)	7 (N)	12
2		11		22		9		22				1
3	2	11	11	9	12	1		6	11	2	9	9
12		12		8		9		23		6		12
8	6	22	1		21	8	20	11	12	22	8	

A B C D̸ E F G H I J K L M N̸ O̸ P Q R S T̸ U V W X Y Z

1	2	3	4	5	6	7	8	9	10	11	12	13
D	O					N				T		

14	15	16	17	18	19	20	21	22	23	24	25	26

TIME

Codeword

Can you crack the code and fill in the crossword grid? Each letter of the alphabet makes at least one appearance in the grid, and is represented by the same number wherever it appears. The four letters we've decoded should help you to identify other letters and words in the grid.

Soundalikes

TIME

Can you complete each of these sentences with two words that sound alike, but are spelled differently?

1 The thief was ____ and tried in ____.

2 We ____ the ____ of cows mooing.

3 ____ ____ stirred the cauldron?

4 Nobody ____ why she poked her ____ in.

58

Splits

Can you rearrange each of these sets of letter blocks into a word?

1 GA LI TOR AL

2 HO LOP NE XY

3 PER ND SA PA

4 DE RM MA ALA

5 NTI TE AL PO

Shape Up

Can you arrange these five-letter shapes into their correct positions in the grid so that ten surnames of film actresses read down the columns?

TIME

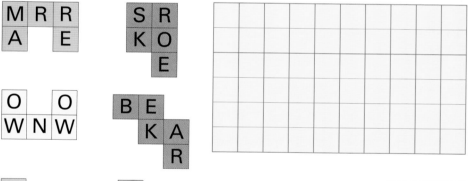

WORKOUT 53

Two of a Kind

Can you sort each set of letter blocks into two words with the same meaning?

1 AN SA AM SE OR IL

2 BIT RB FO OHI ID PR

3 NJ MAG ER CO AN ICI UR

4 EE PE ERS SU OV SE RVI

5 FE IAN ARD DE ER GU ND

Codewords

If HOE=123 and PATH=4561, how quickly can you work out these items found in the garden? You should identify more letters as you go along.

1 4 3 5 6

2 4 2 6 5 6 2

3 7 1 2 2 6 7

4 4 3 6 5 8

5 5 4 4 8 3

Star Turn

Which numbered photograph has been taken?

Fitword

TIME

When all of the listed words have been placed correctly in the grid, which one is left over?

3 letters
Dim
Eye
Icy
Irk
Lie
Pro
Vet
War

4 letters
Dole
Etch

5 letters
Emery
Heady
Huffy
Naval
Renal
~~Rigid~~
Tikka
Wiper

7 letters
Furlong
Seeming
Tactile

8 letters
Regulate
Sightsee

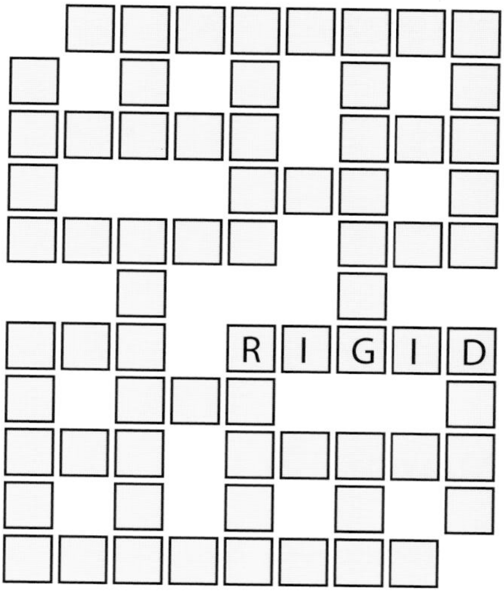

Set Square

TIME

Place one each of the digits 1-9 in the grid to make the sums work. We've put in some of the numbers to start you off. Sums should be solved from left to right, or from top to bottom.

6	÷		+		= 11
+	■	+	■	−	
	−	4	+		= 6
−	■	×	■	÷	
	−		×		= 14
= 10		= 18		= 1	

WORKOUT 55

Pathfinder

 **TIME**

Beginning with CHICORY, and moving up, down, left or right, one letter at a time, can you trace a path of eighteen herbs?

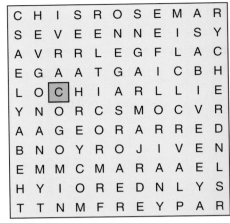

C	H	I	S	R	O	S	E	M	A	R
S	E	V	E	E	N	N	E	I	S	Y
A	V	R	R	L	E	G	F	L	A	C
E	G	A	A	T	G	A	I	C	B	H
L	O	C	H	I	A	R	L	L	I	E
Y	N	O	R	C	S	M	O	C	V	R
A	A	G	E	O	R	A	R	R	E	D
B	N	O	Y	R	O	J	I	V	E	N
E	M	M	C	M	A	R	A	A	E	L
H	Y	I	O	R	E	D	N	L	Y	S
T	T	N	M	F	R	E	Y	P	A	R

Memory Jog

Spend two minutes memorising this list of twenty words, then see how many of them you can recall on a separate piece of paper in another two minutes.

SUITCASE	TREE	SIMPLE	CHANGE
MOUTH	WINDOW	TOWARDS	SHADE
SHIRT	JUMP	KETTLE	TAXI
COLD	SCISSORS	CARRY	IDEA
EARRING	FEATHER	MILK	GRASS

Pyramid

TIME

Each answer except the first uses all the letters – usually in a different order – from the previous answer plus one extra letter.

1 Abbreviation for "King"
2 Egyptian sun god
3 Epoch
4 Attention
5 Provide food
6 Hypnotic state
7 Sure
8 Metal container
9 Wrongdoer

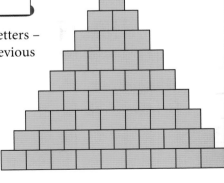

Mind the Gap

Can you place a different three-letter word in the spaces of each row to complete the seven-letter word? Do it correctly, and the shaded letters should spell out a musical instrument.

V	A				C	Y
G	O	R				A
C	A	B				E
A	C				A	T
E	C				S	E
T				K	L	E
E	A	R				R
S				C	I	L

Sudoku

Use your powers of reasoning to place numbers in the grid, so that each row, each column and each 3x3 block contains the numbers 1-9.

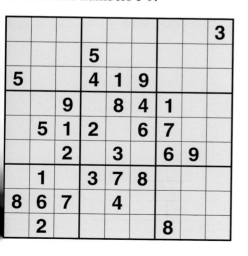

Three in One

The three parts of each clue lead to the same answer word. Can you solve any before you reach the third part?

1 Just • Carnival • Blonde

2 Force • Golf stroke • Go by car

3 Cheek • Narrow opening • Body part

4 Depressed • Snooker ball • Sapphire color

5 Divide • Section • Role

Mini Fit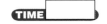

Which one of the listed words won't fit in each of these mini grids?

HAS
PAW
SIP
SKI
WHY

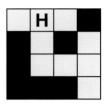

AXE
COD
COX
CUB
EBB

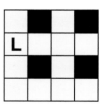

DONE
LAID
LINE
PLEA
SLIP

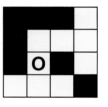

DEER
DROP
PRAM
STEM
TEST

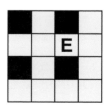

Wordsearch TIME

Hidden in this wordsearch grid are fifteen types of deer.

A	N	T	E	L	O	P	E	K
A	C	R	F	S	D	S	L	T
Z	O	A	H	P	N	E	L	R
E	W	D	R	R	V	O	E	W
N	Z	O	U	I	B	J	Z	R
G	P	E	K	N	B	W	A	I
C	A	C	Y	G	G	O	G	J
Q	U	T	U	B	G	L	U	X
B	Q	H	S	O	M	L	I	L
T	R	A	H	K	D	A	T	K
M	O	O	S	E	E	F	F	C

Vowel Play

Can you replace the missing vowels to complete the names of these insects?

1 M T H   **6** T R M T
2 M S Q T   **7** G N T
3 M D G   **8** C C D
4 B T L   **9** R W G
5 L C S T   **10** P H D

Smart Sums

Try to avoid writing down anything but the final answers to these  calculations... and resist the temptation to count on your fingers!

1. Sides of a square x Lives of a cat
2. Letters of the alphabet + Days in the week
3. Degrees in a right angle ÷ Number of Is in LIAISING
4. Syllables in COSMOPOLITAN + Wives of Henry VIII
5. Legs on a spider – Vowels in TREAD

Mind the Gap

Can you complete the five words in each set by adding the same three-letter word? For example OUR in HLY, FL, FTH (hourly, flour, fourth), and so on.

1 PLD MEN BRLET PLBO ADJNT   4 HY COLL PIER MAROD DISHST

2 PI CHES FSAM CTED CUTES   5 BOR AIST ZIR ANAMA FURST

3 HOG PIG SACH OION SSTER

Kakuro

Simple addition and a bit of logical thinking will solve this one. You must write a digit in each white square so that the digits in each across section add up to the total in the triangle to the left, and the digits in each column add up to the total in the triangle above. 1-9 are the only digits to use and, although you may find a digit repeated in a row, it must not be repeated in the same section. We've solved one section for you.

WORKOUT 59

Arroword

Just follow the arrows to write your answers in the grid. A handful of anagram clues will get you thinking differently.

Narrow-mindedness / Air bed ▼	▼	Flat kitchen surface ▼	▼	Language of South Africa ▼	▼	Tummy muscles ▼	▼	DAN (anag) ▼	▼
►				Of the city ►					
Refuse admittance to (4,3)		Dove's call		Norway's capital		STAB (anag)		RANG (anag)	
►		▼		▼		▼	Gunk ▼		Idiot ▼
Little children ►				Taj Mahal city ►		▼		▼	
				Constrictor snakes ►					
Dribble		Toxins ►							

Futoshiki TIME

Fill the blank squares so that each row and column contains all the numbers 1, 2 and 3. Use the given numbers and the symbols that tell you if the number in the square is larger (>) or smaller (<) than the number next to it.

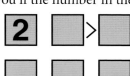

Small Change TIME

Can you change one letter of each of these words to make five new words with a common theme?

1 SKIPPER • VANDAL • SLOG • MALE • BOUT

2 ACE • GRILL • HAMPER • SAD • CLASP

3 FOUL • NIFTY • NICE • OWE • LIGHT

4 FUDGE • CHEW • SET • PIVOT • CLEAVER

5 PAIN • SLOWER • SNOB • HALL • SLEEP

66

Number Jig

Which one of the listed numbers won't fit in each of these mini grids?

364
382
383
423
673

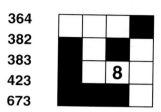

169
257
297
591
927

4825
5738
5743
7352
8375

2114
4162
4461
4661
6412

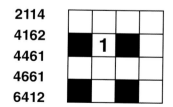

Codewords

If HORSE = 12345 and SNAKE = 46785, how quickly can you work out these creatures? You should identify another letter as you go along.

1 1 5 6

2 1 7 3 5

3 2 9 9 5 3

4 4 9 2 7 9

5 1 2 3 6 5 9

Four by Four

How quickly can you solve this mini crossword?

1	2	3	4
5			
6			
7			

ACROSS
1 Soulful dance music
5 Zone, region
6 Effigy of a god
7 Mystic symbol

DOWN
1 Morally just
2 Official language of Pakistan
3 Noble gas
4 Dark green leafy vegetable

WORKOUT 61

In and Out

TIME

Without changing the order of the letters, add or remove one letter each time to leave a (different) new complete word and put the added or removed letters in their respective boxes to find a fictional US lawyer played by Raymond Burr in a famous TV series reading down the boxes.

SPORT		CAP	
CHAT		WHEAT	
CHAT		ROUSE	
THERM		CURSE	
ERIE		CHANT	

Four by Four

TIME

How quickly can you solve this mini crossword?

	1	2	3	4
5				
6				
7				

ACROSS
1 Bundle of hay
5 Leave the stage
6 Smart ___, wise guy
7 Fishing-net material

DOWN
1 Roof support
2 Rod joining two wheels
3 Fibs
4 Engrave

Splits

TIME

Can you rearrange each of these sets of letter blocks into a word?

1 CL LM FI ING

2 RVI TE IN EW

3 RE FU TU RNI

4 IRS AY HA PR

5 OI RQU TU SE

Mini Jigsaw

Fit the pieces in the grid to spell out a country in each row.

| T U | C E | F R |
| N O | D A | C A |

| P R | E Y | A N |
| L A | A Y | N A |

| U S | R K | C Y |
| N D | R W | P O |

	1					
	2			A		
	3					
	4				A	
	5					
	6		A			

Killer Sudoku

TIME

The normal rules of Sudoku apply. Place a digit from 1-9 in each empty square so that each row, column and 3x3 block contains all the digits from 1-9. In addition, the digits in each inner shape (marked by dots) must add up to the number in the top corner of that box. No digit can be repeated within an inner shape.

18			12		20		6	16
	9		17		10			
18		24	7				13	
				18				7
8	11		12		11		17	
		3		25		16		
10								22
16	5		18	16			4	
	13 8	5			3			

WORKOUT 63

Initials TIME

If ITHOTN (Oscar-winning film) is *IN THE HEAT OF THE NIGHT*, what do these initials represent?

1 HAT (Cake decoration)

2 KUA (Sitcom)

3 AYLT (Elvis song)

4 ROTLA (Harrison Ford film)

5 BIACS (Clumsy person)

Missing Link TIME

The three words in each clue have a fourth word in common, and that's your answer. For example, the clue "Moon • Navy • Royal" gives the answer BLUE (blue moon, navy blue, royal blue). Write each answer in the grid, and the shaded column will reveal a constellation.

1 Heat • Length • Mexican

2 Door • File • Thumb

3 Birth • Down • Question

4 Jump • Knee • Light

5 Bare • Step • Stool

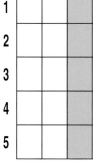

Fix Six TIME

The six rivers listed will fit into this pattern of six adjoining hexagons. All are entered clockwise from a triangle to be discovered. Adjoining triangles always contain the same letter. The **B** gives you a start.

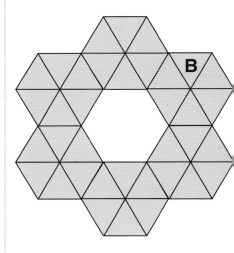

COQUET	KENNET
DANUBE	THAMES
GANGES	TIGRIS

70

Wild Words

What well-known phrases and expressions are suggested by these word pictures?

1 **ARREST YOU'RE**

2 EVER EVER
EVER EVER

3 **HACASHND**

4 **0,2,3,4,5**

Elimination

All but two of the listed words fall into one of the four categories. Put these leftover words together, and what new phrase do they make?

CATEGORIES Gemstones • Words meaning DRAW • Words following BREAD (e.g., Bin) • Parts of the face

Brow	Line	Raffle	Crumb	Sauce	Sketch
Pull	Band	Jade	Attract	Amber	Lip
Jet	Diamond	Chin	Opal	Brass	
Nose	Winner	Stick	Tie	Cheek	

Copycats

Choose the answer that best copies the pattern.

LEFT is to RIGHT as RIGHT is to: Correct • Angle • Proper • Wrong • Hand

HARE is to LEVERET as EEL is to: Jelly • Elver • Heifer • Snake • Fish

SHAPE is to TRIANGLE as PIANO is to: Key • Tune • Pedal • Heavy • Upright

8361 is to 1863 as 2794 is to: 4297 • 7924 • 4279 • 7249 • 7429

VEGETARIAN is to HAM as VEGAN is to: Milk • Apple • Peanut • Rice • Lentil

WORKOUT 65

Wordsearch

How quickly can you find the five themed words in each grid?

FRUIT

A	N	A	N	A	B	P
O	P	Y	I	H	A	P
I	R	R	C	W	A	N
U	C	A	I	P	I	E
B	E	L	A	C	G	K
P	W	Y	X	S	O	V
J	A	H	D	K	M	T

GALLERY

B	A	R	L	S	E	S
H	K	O	Q	U	F	A
M	J	T	T	R	A	V
U	C	A	Y	G	R	N
E	T	R	Z	X	V	A
S	W	U	I	O	P	C
P	I	C	T	U	R	E

Vowel Play

Can you replace the missing vowels to complete the names of these fabrics?

1 SLK   4 RYN   7 PLD   10 SD

2 DNM   5 TWD   8 LNN

3 WL   6 PSLY   9 NGR

Cell Blocks

Fill the grid by drawing blocks along the gridlines. Each block must be square or rectangular and must contain the number of squares indicated by the digit inside it. Each block must contain only one digit.

	3		1		2
2	5				
			8		
3				4	
		3			3
				2	

72

Sudoku　TIME

Place a number in each empty square so that each row, each column and each 2x2 block contains all the numbers from 1-4.

	4		2
2		4	
	1		3
3		1	

		1	2
	1		4
	3	2	

2	3	1	4
4	1	3	2

Add Up　TIME

If the number in each circle is the sum of the two below it, how quickly can you figure out the top number? Try this one in your head, before writing anything down.

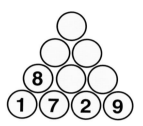

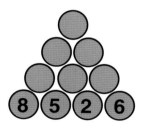

73

WORKOUT 67

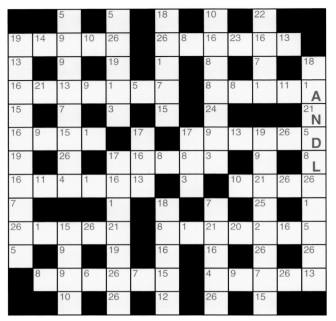

Codeword

Can you crack the code and fill in the crossword grid? Each letter of the alphabet makes at least one appearance in the grid, and is represented by the same number wherever it appears. The four letters we've decoded should help you to identify other letters and words in the grid.

A̶ B C D̶ E F G H I J K L̶ M N̶ O P Q R S T U V W X Y Z

1	2	3	4	5	6	7	8	9	10	11	12	13
A				**D**			**L**					
14	15	16	17	18	19	20	21	22	23	24	25	26
							N					

Spot the Sum

TIME

In each of these boxes, one of the numbers is the sum of two others. Can you spot the sum?

1

7   32   20   1   9
4   15   34   22

3

24   12   4   37   18
30   9   29   23

2

33   18   5   12   29
37   11   3   31

4

6   19   39   15   29
8   35   26   30

74

Scramble

What countries can be made from each of these sets of scrambled letters?

TIME

1 PURE

2 WEALS

3 OLD PAN

4 MEG RYAN

5 REGALIA

6 A THIN LAD

7 ABSORB AD

8 MOON RACE

Tennis Match

Which numbered photograph has been taken?

TIME

Futoshiki

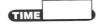
TIME

Fill the blank squares so that each row and column contains all the numbers 1, 2, 3 and 4. Use the given numbers and the symbols that tell you if the number in the square is larger (>) or smaller (<) than the number next to it.

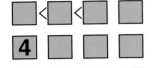

Letter Sequence

TIME

What letter should replace the question-mark in these sequences?

1 A, D, G, J, ?

2 X, V, T, R, ?

3 Y, ?, P, M, K

4 P, D, ?, E, N, F, M

5 J, F, M, A, M, J, ?

Disavowel

TIME

Can you complete this puzzle by adding all the vowels?
There are 13 As, 16 Es, 7 Is, 6 Os and 1 U in the puzzle.

R		D		S	H	■	H		C	K
	R		M		■	B		R		N
S		M	P	L			P		R	
P			L		D		P	L		
■	S	■	Y	■		C		■		D
D	■	J	■		T		N		■	
	K		P		■		S			R
C		C		D		■		T	■	
	N	K	S	■	L		T	H		L
L			T	H		R	■		W	
	■	L		■				R	L	S

Fitword

When all of the listed words have been placed correctly in the grid, which one is left over?

3 letters
Chi
Cob
Eat
Ops
Out
Rig
Tod

4 letters
Abut
Debt
Sigh
Sour

5 letters
~~Again~~
Bulge
Heaps

Revel
Tread
Vying

7 letters
Circled
Origami

8 letters
Fretting
Peculiar

Set Square

Place one each of the digits 1-9 in the grid to make the sums work. We've put in some of the numbers to start you off. Sums should be solved from left to right, or from top to bottom.

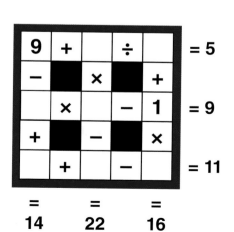

77

Pathfinder

Beginning with WOOD, and moving up, down, left or right, one letter at a time, can you trace a path of twenty-two golfing words?

E	A	E	G	G	E	R	Y	D	E	R
S	G	L	O	D	E	W	G	A	L	C
S	O	R	L	F	B	I	R	D	F	U
O	U	D	R	A	U	O	R	I	E	P
R	G	O	R	Z	N	R	E	K	A	C
T	H	F	E	A	D	E	L	N	D	D
A	B	L	A	H	F	A	O	U	B	Y
D	O	O	W	Y	A	I	H	G	T	I
G	E	L	L	A	W	R	I	N	C	P
R	R	B	M	B	H	A	W	S	H	P
E	E	N	U	A	G	N	D	I	C	A

Memory Jog

You have two minutes to study the list of twenty words. Then give yourself another two minutes to write as many of the words as you can recall on a separate piece of paper.

FREE	SNAIL	SAUNA	SWIM	ECHO
CARPET	LETTER	FENCE	WINE	ZERO
KEYBOARD	PALM	BABY	MAYBE	EARWAX
JAM	DREAM	BANANA	COWBOY	INK

Pairs

Pair off 24 of the listed words to form twelve "double-barreled" words and rearrange the letters of the two words left over to reveal a pop group or a position of desperate difficulty.

BLACK	BREAKFAST	CLOTH	CYCLIST	DRESSING
DRIVING	FEED	FRENCH	HEAD	MARKET
PARTY	SPOON	START	TIRED	
BREAK	HOT	COFFEE	DAY	
ENGLISH	GREEN	DOG	LICENCE	
SCHOOL	STAIRS	TABLE	TRICK	

Honeycomb

TIME

Write the six-letter answers clockwise round their respective cell-numbers, starting at the arrowed cell. On completion, you will find that the unclued answers (10 and 11) will reveal a former Tory Chancellor of the Exchequer.

1 Distant (3,3)
2 Captor's demand
3 Go without food
4 Have in mind
5 Leisurely country walk
6 Ill-will
7 Frequently encountered
8 He shrinks from danger
9 Strand of pasta in chicken soup

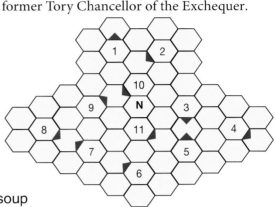

Sudoku

TIME

Use your powers of reasoning to place numbers in the grid, so that each row, each column and each 3x3 block contains the numbers 1-9.

		9						8
			8	5	4			
		8	2	3				9
	7	1					9	6
			6	1	2			
4	6						1	8
1				9	6	7		
		5	7	4				
8					3			

Mobile Code

TIME

If MAPLE is 62753 on this phone keypad, what trees have the following numbers?

1 625
2 7463
3 23327
4 24724
5 945569
6 222242

Word Builder

Using the nine letters provided, can you answer these clues? Every answer must include the highlighted letter R. What spread uses all nine letters?

G	I	A
R	R	M
E	A	N

5 Letters
Rule over a country
Dirt
Sports stadium
Colliery worker
Irate emotion
Single piece of sand

6 Letters
European language
Stay behind
Yacht harbor
Italian designer label
Page border
Optical illusion

7 Letters
Person in charge
Item of jewelry

8 Letters
Wedding

Wordsearch

Hidden in this wordsearch grid are fifteen cooking methods.

P	Z	U	R	V	A	Y	Q	S
R	B	A	K	O	R	Y	M	A
T	H	A	H	F	A	P	J	U
C	S	B	R	A	I	S	E	T
W	H	A	C	B	R	F	T	E
E	C	R	O	S	E	K	A	B
T	A	W	D	T	M	C	T	G
S	O	D	D	I	M	C	U	B
M	P	O	L	E	I	L	O	E
J	M	A	E	T	S	I	N	B
G	R	I	L	L	L	G	X	W

Opposites Attract

Can you sort each set of letter blocks into two words with opposite meanings?

1 UR SWE SO ET

2 HT OSE LO TIG

3 RO AK NG ST WE

4 CE IT RAN EX ENT

5 VE PE AP EX CHE NSI

Memory Quiz

Here's a quiz to see how much attention you're really paying to your surroundings. No peeping!

1 What is the chemical symbol for iron?

2 What is the cube root of 64?

3 Supercede – is that the correct spelling?

4 In which hand does the Statue of Liberty hold the torch?

5 What is the color of the McDonalds logo?

6 On a keyboard, is the V or B further left?

Smart Sums

Try to avoid writing down anything but the final answers to these calculations... no counting on fingers allowed either!

1 Letters in CAMSHAFT – Syllables in CARBURETTOR

2 Days in September ÷ Es in BEEKEEPER

3 Leaves on a lucky clover x Vowels in MOZAMBIQUE

4 Minutes in an hour – Consonants in POLYTHENE

5 Squares on a chessboard + Legs on a tripod

Kakuro

Simple addition and a bit of logical thinking will solve this one. You must write a digit in each white square so that the digits in each across section add up to the total in the triangle to the left, and the digits in each column add up to the total in the triangle above. 1-9 are the only digits to use and, although you may find a digit repeated in a row, it must not be repeated in the same section. We've solved one section for you.

Arroword

Just follow the arrows to write your answers in the grid. A handful of anagram clues will get you thinking differently.

(Of the night sky) twinkly ▼	Number in a duet ▼		Soil fertiliser ▼		Pastry dish	▼	TREASON (anag) ▼	— interest personal stake
Haulage line (3-4) ▶				▼			CLEAR (anag)
Part of a curve	Pacify	Chop finely ▶				▼	
▶	▼	Scottish river	PALES (anag) ▶				
Wireless ▶		▼			Shabby odds and ends ▶		
			Sleeper's grunt! ▶				
▶ Jeremy —, talk-show host	Turn to liquid ▶				Garnet colour		

Staircase

When the seven composers are correctly placed along the horizontal rows, the letters in the diagonal "staircase" will yield an eighth.

BRITTEN
DVORAK
ELGAR
GLINKA
MAHLER
ROSSINI
STRAUSS

Small Change

Can you change one letter of each of these words to make five new words with a common theme?

1 BARGE • BUG • VASE • CHOPPING • PASSIVE

2 PELMET • PULP • BAKE • RICE • MEDAL

3 GAMBLE • MATCH • WALL • STRUM • HIRE

4 STEAL • CORK • PEACH • DIMMER • PRY

Number Jig

Which one of the listed numbers won't fit in each of these mini grids?

259
752
792
799
925

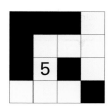

123
133
217
371
721

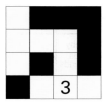

4896
6884
6948
8496
9464

3517
3578
5131
8317
8573

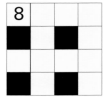

Splits

Can you rearrange each of these sets of letter blocks into a word?

1 GE PA ID RTR
2 NG HI MET SO
3 ART QU LY ER
4 SE TH OR CAR
5 LE OZ MBO BA

Four by Four

How quickly can you solve this mini crossword?

	1	2	3	4
5				
6				
7				

ACROSS
1 Suddenly run off
5 Neighbourhood
6 Harsh grating sound
7 Otherwise

DOWN
1 Starkers
2 Spoken test
3 Not as much
4 Record on video

Niners

Form four nine-letter words using all twelve listed "syllables" (without altering the order of the letters in each "syllable"). Then enter them in the grid in the right order to reveal a Scottish family group reading down the left-hand column.

APA	CAL	CHE
ERI	ENT	LAB
MIS	NTH	NUM
RTM	TRY	YRI

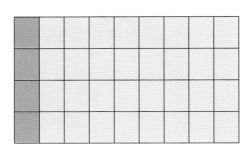

All Fours

Fit the four listed words across the rows of the grid so that four more words read downwards.

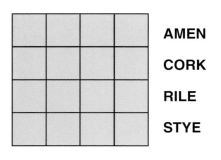

AMEN

CORK

RILE

STYE

Box Wise

Can you place the three-letter groups in the boxes, so that neighbouring boxes always make a six-letter word, like PAR-DON or DON-ATE? We've placed one group to start you off.

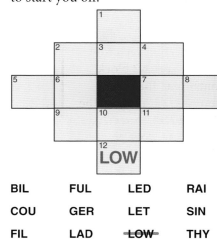

BIL	FUL	LED	RAI
COU	GER	LET	SIN
FIL	LAD	~~LOW~~	THY

84

Mini Jigsaw

TIME

Fit the pieces in the grid to spell out a animal in each row.

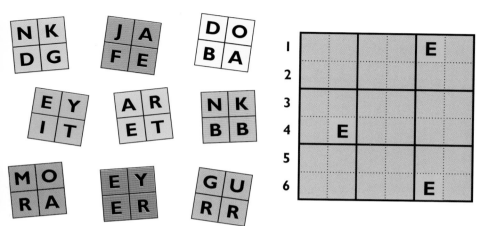

Killer Sudoku

TIME

The normal rules of Sudoku apply. Place a digit from 1-9 in each empty square so that each row, column and 3x3 block contains all the digits from 1-9. In addition, the digits in each inner shape (marked by dots) must add up to the number in the top corner of that box. No digit can be repeated within an inner shape.

Futoshiki

Fill the blank squares so that each row and column contains all the numbers 1, 2 and 3. Use the given numbers and the symbols that tell you if the number in the square is larger (>) or smaller (<) than the number next to it.

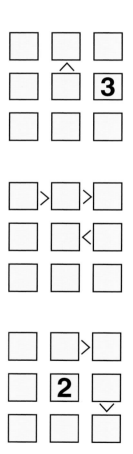

Word Builder

Using the nine letters provided, can you answer these clues? Every answer must include the highlighted letter N. What major port of SE Asia uses all nine letters?

R	I	E
O	N	P
S	A	G

5 Letters
Kitchen garment
Part of a fork
Sigh loudly
Backbone

6 Letters
Fruit
Take no notice of
Higher in rank
Racing bird
Clergyman
Persuade to take part (4,2)

7 Letters
Freeloader
Taking place outside (4-3)
Prehistoric period (4,3)
Extremely hot

8 Letters
Make preparations for

Fare's Fair

Find two words of the same sound but different spelling to satisfy each two-element clue, then decide which of the pair goes where in the grid to discover the Christian name of Mr. Marr, who presents BBC's *Sunday AM*, reading down the arrowed column.

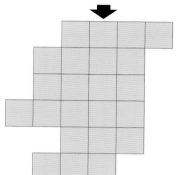

Painful tool

Trapped at judicial building

Moisture is about to arrive

Sheet of glass's dull ache

Lift up sunbeams

Team moaned

Splits

Can you rearrange each of these sets of letter blocks into a word?

1 WE UN AR DER

2 EN ER GRE EV

3 MU TY NI COM

4 LE ATH CS TI

5 RE NIA TU MI

Memory Jog

Give yourself two minutes to memorise this list of words – thirty this time! How many of them can you recall on a separate piece of paper in another two minutes?

PLIERS	CARAVAN	ARMCHAIR	CIDER	GUITAR	CIRCLE
BOX	GOAL	APRICOT	TRAIN	SHOE	HAPPY
PUZZLE	BRIDGE	SCHOOL	LEFT	TOFFEE	TOWEL
ANKLE	FAN	FUNNY	SAUCER	FLOOR	
STREAM	UNDER	MASCOT	JUST		
TYPE	GLITTER	LIZARD			

Memory Jog

Spend two minutes memorising this list of twenty words, then
see how many of them you can recall on a separate piece of paper.

MONKEYS	TALKING	SPRY	ROLL
THOUGHT	IDEA	SELL	QUILT
SONG	PASTY	WORLD	WAGGISH
LIVING	FLAVOR	LIKEABLE	CAMP
WAGON	ACCENT	MYSELF	STARSHIP

Logical

Try solving this little logical problem in your head before putting pen to paper.

Tom, Dick and Harry are each planning their weekend camping trips to the Lake District, Peak District and Yorkshire Dales. The most important part of the planning was which luxury to take with them – brandy, chocolate or tea bags.

Dick planned his trip to the Peak District, and his luxury wasn't brandy. Tom's luxury was chocolate, and his trip wasn't to the Yorkshire Dales. Who went where and what was their luxury?

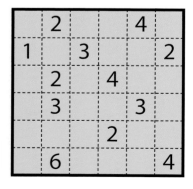

Cell Blocks

Fill the grid by drawing blocks along the gridlines. Each block must be square or rectangular and must contain the number of squares indicated by the digit inside it. Each block must contain only one digit.

Sudoku

TIME

Place a number in each empty square so that each row, each column and each 2x2 block contains all the numbers from 1-4.

4			2
	2	4	
	4	3	
3			4

1			2
	2	1	
	1	3	
3			1

	3	4	
	1	3	
	4	2	
	2	1	

Wordsearch

TIME

How quickly can you find the seven themed words in each grid?

HORSE

P	Y	E	K	C	O	J
E	U	T	S	R	B	R
L	P	R	U	Z	E	E
D	J	O	R	T	W	I
D	E	T	N	I	N	N
A	A	A	C	H	T	S
S	C	J	U	M	P	S

CHEST

C	K	N	U	R	T	K
O	V	B	L	I	B	N
F	B	O	X	A	X	E
F	C	A	S	K	E	T
E	C	K	J	U	O	A
R	E	P	M	A	H	R
T	A	Q	E	T	M	C

NUT

L	W	P	A	G	X	A
I	A	E	P	V	L	J
Z	L	C	H	M	E	F
A	N	A	O	S	Z	B
R	S	N	W	Y	A	I
B	D	H	P	K	H	C
M	O	N	K	E	Y	Z

Codeword

TIME ____

Can you crack the code and fill in the crossword grid? Each letter of the alphabet makes at least one appearance in the grid, and is represented by the same number wherever it appears. The four letters we've decoded should help you to identify other letters and words in the grid.

A B C D̷ E̷ F G H I J K L M N O P Q R̷ S T̷ U V W X Y Z

1	2	3	4	5	6	7	8	9	10	11	12	13
14	15	16	17	18	19	20	21	22	23	24	25	26
	D			T	E	R						

So Complete

TIME ____

Complete each trio of words with a common letter. The five letters will form the answer word. Where there is a choice of completing letter, you must decide which is needed.

WIL_	WI_E	I_LE	____
WA_N	W_EN	WEA_	____
DE_R	MO_T	AL_S	____
CA_E	_ORD	LEA_	____
_EST	MA_E	SE_T	____

Spot the Sum

TIME

In each of these boxes, one of the numbers is the sum of two others. Can you spot the sum?

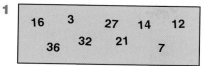

1

| 16 | 3 | 27 | 14 | 12 |
| 36 | 32 | 21 | 7 | |

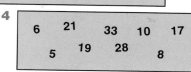

3

| 23 | 4 | 11 | 18 | 36 |
| 2 | 37 | 8 | 32 | |

2

| 28 | 1 | 15 | 31 | 24 |
| 12 | 5 | 18 | 9 | |

4

| 6 | 21 | 33 | 10 | 17 |
| 5 | 19 | 28 | 8 | |

Pieceword

TIME

With the help of the Across clues only, can you fit the 16 pieces into their correct positions in the empty grid (which, when completed, will exhibit a symmetrical pattern)?

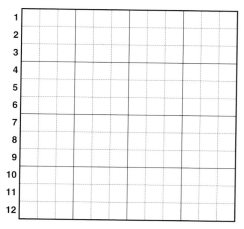

ACROSS

1 Virtuous

2 Almost, approximately

3 Acclimatised

4 Baffling mystery

5 Crisp lustrous silk

6 Game played with an oval ball

7 Sludge

8 ___ colors, red, blue and yellow

9 Fairy cave

10 Criminal's lever

11 Take-off

12 Poem with fourteen lines

91

Mix-Up

These letters in each case can be rearranged to spell something either famously yellow or blue in a song or film title.

Sub marine

1 RUBMANISE
2 TEVVEL *velvet*
3 VERIR *River*
4 SLORL COREY *Rolls*
5 THOLE *Clothe blue Bell*
6 WAIHAI *Hawaii*
7 NOMO *moon*
8 KCRIB DORA *Brick Road*
9 EROS FO TAXES *Rose of Tx*
10 DUESE EHOSS *Suede shoes*

Four by Four

How quickly can you solve this mini crossword?

1 L	2 G	3	4
5 A	O		
6 C	N		
7 C	P	C	N

ACROSS
1 Lionise
5 Crooked
6 Animal pen
7 Observed

DOWN
1 Shoe fastener
2 Absent
3 Strong desire
4 Color-stained

Memory Jog

Here's a good test of your short-term memory. We've got a filled word square on the left, and a partially filled square on the right. The words reading down in the square on the left are made up from the letters of the words "NUMBER" and "LETTER." Cover up the square on the right, then spend two minutes memorising the words in the square on the left. When your two minutes are up cover the square and then see if you can recreate it in the partially-filled square on the right.

B	M	R	T	B	E
U	U	U	U	U	N
T	T	M	R	T	T
L	T	B	R	T	R
E	E	L	E	E	E
R	R	E	T	R	E

	M			B	E
					N
			R		
		B	R		
				E	

Fitword

TIME

When all of the listed words have been placed correctly in the grid, which one is left over?

3 letters
Ago
Ion

Piece
Pined
Spite

Tampered
Vagabond
War paint

4 letters
Ibis
Tidy

7 letters
Illness
Morello

9 letters
Balancing
Propelled

5 letters
Dregs

8 letters
~~Proposer~~
Scolding

Six Pack

TIME

Can you place digits in the empty triangles, so that the numbers in each hexagon add up to 25? Only single digits between 1 and 9 can be used, and no two numbers in any hexagon may be the same.

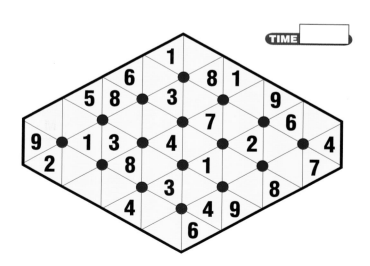

93

Pathfinder

TIME ☐

Beginning with *THE BOYFRIEND*, and moving up, down, left or right, one letter at a time, can you trace a path of fourteen musicals?

O	D	P	P	Y	R	G	N	N	O	I
O	A	I	O	P	A	M	I	K	E	L
N	G	N	O	K	L	A	I	R	H	T
G	I	S	L	H	A	H	R	I	T	Y
O	R	B	L	O	M	A	A	H	C	T
D	S	P	E	A	M	M	I	A	E	E
S	F	N	Y	M	E	A	M	G	W	S
D	U	N	F	A	C	C	I	R	E	E
O	T	O	T	O	G	A	H	T	A	S
O	H	I	N	M	N	D	C	H	E	B
W	E	E	M	A	E	I	R	F	Y	O

Soundalikes

TIME ☐

Can you complete each of these sentences with two words that sound alike, but are spelled differently?

1 She ___ the ___ and improved version would work.
2 The walkers clambered over the ___ in some ___.
3 "___ be proud to walk you down the ___," said the father to his daughter on her wedding day.
4 The fishmonger advised the body-builder to eat more ___ if he wanted bigger *mus clos*

Copycats

TIME ☐

Choose the answer that best copies the pattern.

FISH is to HERRING as BIRD is to: Tail • Feather • Fly • Duck • Beak

11 is to 121 as 13 is to: 169 • 213 • 131 • 193 • 129

CARE is to CASE as DALE is to: Dare • Dame • Dole • Pale • Date

DRUM is to STICK as VIOLIN is to: String • Peg • Bow • Fiddle • Pluck

Buzz Off

TIME

Which two pictures are identical?

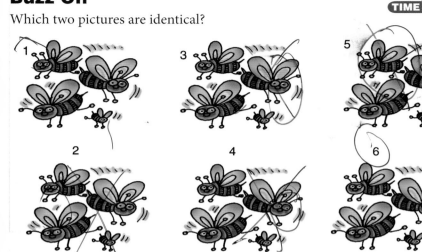

Sudoku

TIME

Use your powers of reasoning to place numbers in the grid, so that each row, each column and each 3x3 block contains the numbers 1-9.

			2			3		7
			8		3	4	9	6
		3			9			1
6	3				4			
					6		8	
	5	9	3	1				
5	8							
	2			4				8
1	9	4				7		

Splits

TIME

Can you rearrange each of these sets of letter blocks into a word?

Concorhed

1 CON ED CE RN

Machinist

2 NI MA ST CHI

Beautiful

3 UL AU BE TIF

Boulevard

4 VA BOU RD LE

Pageantry

5 AN PA TRY GE

carapathi
Pageaintry
chimanist

Lettersets

Complete the crossword grid using the letters listed for each row and column. Cracking this one relies on anagram-solving and cross-referencing between Across and Down words.

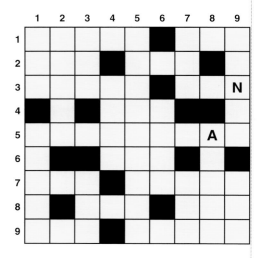

ACROSS

1 AABDLORS
2 ACEEEFL
3 AEFGNSSU
4 ADPTT
5 ADEERSTYY
6 AEERR
7 AAIMRSST
8 COOOPRT
9 EEENNTVW

DOWN

1 AAEGNRSY
2 ACEERTU
3 EELOSTW
4 AAEPST
5 ADEEEPRST
6 ALMRTV
7 CDEFFIO
8 AANORRS
9 BDENOSTY

Wordsearch

Hidden in this wordsearch grid are fifteen cheeses.

Futoshiki

Fill the blank squares so that each row and column contains all the numbers 1, 2 and 3. Use the given numbers and the symbols that tell you if the number in the square is larger (>) or smaller (<) than the number next to it.

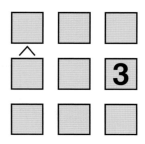

Smart Sums

Try to avoid writing down anything but the final answers to these calculations... and resist the temptation to count on your fingers!

1 Vowels in ALABASTER + ounces in 2lbs

2 Hours in March and May – days in January, June and July

3 Top number on a dartboard + usable squares on a Checker board

4 Syllables in CORONET x corners on 2 dice

5 5p pieces needed to make £2.55 – age you become eligible to vote

Small Change

Can you change one letter of each of these words to make five new words with a common theme?

1 SWAP • FRIDGE • MUMMY • POWER • WHISK

2 DAIRY • AMP • TRILL • ELK • PERT

3 BARE • ROOST • FRILL • STEM • POUCH

4 BEACON • DEAR • MERGER • BEAGLE • CASTOR

Kakuro

Simple addition and a bit of logical thinking will solve this one. You must write a digit in each white square so that the digits in each across section add up to the total in the triangle to the left, and the digits in each column add up to the total in the triangle above. 1-9 are the only digits to use and, although you may find a digit repeated in a row, it must not be repeated in the same section. We've solved one section for you.

	4	3		20	23	6	8		
4	3	1	13 6					12	16
45									
		19					17		

WORKOUT 91

Arroword

Just follow the arrows to write your answers in the grid. A handful of anagram clues will get you thinking differently.

Noisy party HOSE (anag) ▼	▼	Fiendish	▼	Deprive of life or vitality	▼	Mr Stallone's nickname	▼	Remains after burning	▼
▶				Does nothing ▶					
Heathen		Weapon		MODE (anag)		Village People hit (inits)		Rod with magical properties	
▶		▼		▼		▼	Organ controlling balance ▼	▼	— Moines, Iowa's capital ▼
NUDE (anag) ▶				Fermented honey drink ▶		▼		▼	
				Bamboo stick ▶					
In music, a double note ▶	People lacking courage ▶								

Vowel Play

Can you replace the missing vowels to complete the names of these sports?

1 J D
2 P L
3 R B C S
4 K R T
5 B X N G
6 D V N G
7 R G B Y
8 T N N S
9 R C H R Y
10 F T B L L

Two of a Kind

Can you sort each set of letter blocks into two words with the same meaning?

1 CO NU RY ENT NV NNE

2 DE NS TE ER BE CO LI RA ID

3 SU RE SH UP OT LT

4 FU NG IR UL MI EF

5 GI NG ER LA LI UG GG HT

Fix Six

The six items of food listed will fit into this pattern of six adjoining hexagons. All are entered clockwise from a triangle to be discovered. Adjoining triangles always contain the same letter. The Q gives you a start.

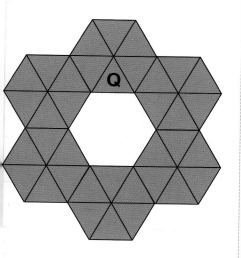

CANAPE   HUMMUS

CHEESE   QUICHE

HAGGIS   SALAMI

Mobile Code

If YORK is 9675 on this phone keypad, what county towns have the following numbers?

1 33729

2 87876

3 393837

4 4779424

5 8286866

Initials

If ITHOTN (Oscar-winning film) is *IN THE HEAT OF THE NIGHT*, what do these initials represent?

1 TVQ (Monarch's nickname)

2 TKAM (Classic US novel and film)

3 TWTIA (ABBA hit)

4 KHAC (Ealing comedy)

5 NABNALB (Proverb)

WORKOUT 93

Mind the Gap

Can you place a well-known three-letter word in the spaces of each row to complete the seven-letter word? Do it correctly, and the shaded letters should spell out something to eat.

D	E				I	R
A	L				E	D
G	N				E	R
S				M	E	R
E	N				C	E
E	D	U				E
T				A	N	I
H	A	U				R

Four by Four

How quickly can you solve this mini crossword?

1	2	3	4
5			
6			
7			

ACROSS
1 Small ship
5 Arab prince
6 Yield (to another)
7 Joint of the leg

DOWN
1 At your ___ and call, at your service
2 Prophetic sign
3 Adviser
4 Plant with a trunk

Box Wise

Can you place the three-letter groups in the boxes, so that neighbouring boxes always make a six-letter word, like PAR-DON or DON-ATE? We've placed one group to start you off.

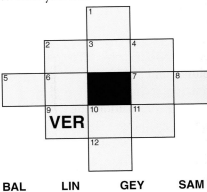

BAL	LIN	GEY	SAM
BIL	LOW	MAR	SER
LET	GER	PUR	~~VER~~

Mini Jigsaw

Fit the pieces in the grid to spell out a sport in each row.

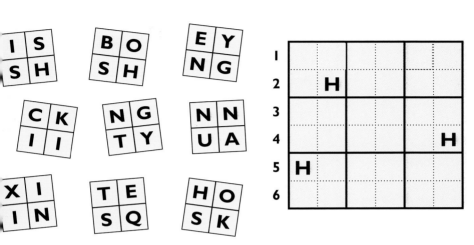

Killer Sudoku

The normal rules of sudoku apply. Place a digit from 1-9 in each empty square so that each row, column and 3x3 block contains all the digits from 1-9. In addition, the digits in each inner shape (marked by dots) must add up to the number in the top corner of that box. No digit can be repeated within an inner shape.

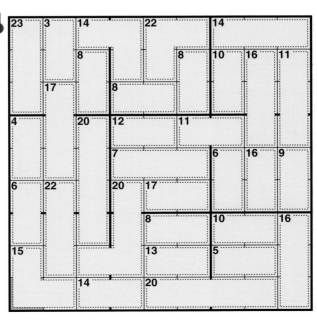

Word Builder TIME

Using the nine letters provided, can you answer these clues? Every answer must include the highlighted letter C. Which artisan uses all nine letters?

R	E	N
A	C	T
R	E	P

5 Letters
Lack of hostility
Mother-of-pearl
Put up
Frolic
Type of nut
Storage box

6 Letters
Of late
Professional life
Floor covering
Make
Middle
Drink of the gods

7 Letters
Row of houses
Perform again
Go over again

Number Jig TIME

Which one of the listed numbers won't fit in each of these mini grids

689
768
879
897
987

327
352
435
478
528

5678
5768
6785
6857
8675

1212
2112
2123
3232
3322

In and Out

TIME

Without changing the order of the letters, add or remove one letter each time to leave a (different) new complete word and put the added or removed letters in their respective boxes to find the envoy who was a hostage in Lebanon from 1987 until 1991 reading down the boxes.

SEAM ☐ TON ☐
CRAM ☐ TAUT ☐
TROUGH ☐ DEAL ☐
SPRAIN ☐ SLEIGHT ☐
TANS ☐ CREATE ☐

Set Square

TIME

Place one each of the digits 1-9 in the grid to make the sums work. We've put in some of the numbers to start you off. Sums should be solved from left to right, or from top to bottom.

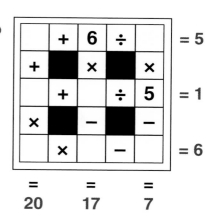

	+	6	÷		= 5
+		×		×	
	+		÷	5	= 1
×		−		−	
	×		−		= 6
= 20		= 17		= 7	

Elimination

TIME

All but two of the listed words fall into one of the four categories. Put these leftover words together, and what word do they make?

CATEGORIES Words that follow "Sand" • Synonyms of "Chasm" • Trees • Aircraft

Sycamore	Castle	Banyan	Gorge	Cliff	Bag
Airship	Crevasse	Paper	Beech	Crater	Jet
Pit	Balloon	Hanger	Helicopter	Storm	
Abyss	Ash	Glider	Willow	Ravine	

Wordsearch

How quickly can you find the seven themed words in each grid?

SUN ____

B	R	S	Y	T	O	F
J	A	E	H	T	A	B
I	W	G	W	I	K	E
L	I	R	T	O	N	H
L	N	O	E	Z	L	E
T	G	O	S	C	X	F
P	D	F	Y	A	D	S

____ MOON

O	L	Z	T	F	A	P
W	L	Y	S	D	G	A
E	U	W	E	N	V	P
H	F	U	V	N	M	E
U	L	C	R	J	O	R
B	F	L	A	H	B	H
N	I	T	H	Q	P	L

Splits

Can you rearrange each of these sets of letter blocks into a word?

1 RA MI BLE SE

2 ST HY CS ERI

3 TE AC HU PAR

4 ES TI AL SEN

5 ARB ST RD OA

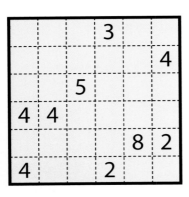

Cell Blocks

Fill the grid by drawing blocks along the gridlines. Each block must be square or rectangular and must contain the number of squares indicated by the digit inside it. Each block must contain only one digit.

Sudoku

TIME

Place a number in each empty square so that each row, each column and each 2x2 block contains all the numbers from 1-4.

	1	2	
3			1
1			2
	3	1	

	4	1	
1			4
3			1
	1	3	

3			1
	1	3	
	4	1	
1			4

Add Up

TIME

If the number in each circle is the sum of the two below it, how quickly can you figure out the top number? Try this one in your head, before writing anything down.

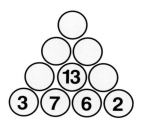

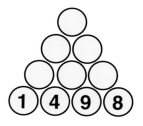

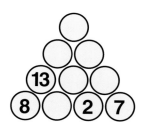

TIME

Codeword

Can you crack the code and fill in the crossword grid? Each letter of the alphabet makes at least one appearance in the grid, and is represented by the same number wherever it appears. The four letters we'v decoded should help you to identify other letters and words in the grid.

Copycats

TIME

Choose the answer that best copies the pattern.

$^1/_8$ **is to 0.125 as** $^2/_5$ **is to:** 0.25 • 0.33 • 0.4 • 0.525 • 0.6

PANEL is to PLANE as CAVER is to: Crave • Caper • Cover • Carve • Caves

GLUTTONY is to SIN as CHARITY is to: Love • Kindness • Virtue • Justice • Generosity

TWENTY is to CHINA as THIRTY is to: Gold • Hong Kong • Ruby • Japan • Pearl

BULGE is to GLUE as PARTY is to: Tory • Tray • Trap • Rave • Ball

Memory Jog

Spend two minutes memorising this list of twenty words, then see how many of them you can recall on a separate piece of paper in another two minutes.

FIFTY	FAR	ACCEPT	LAUDABLE
OPEN	DECIMAL	ORIGIN	PLENTIFUL
WILL	REVISION	STOLEN	ENDING
PROBABLE	AUDIBLE	REALLY	ORANGE
TIME	SCREEN	DELAY	VENISON

Shape Up

Can you arrange these five-letter shapes into their correct positions in the grid so that ten London boroughs read down the columns?

TIME

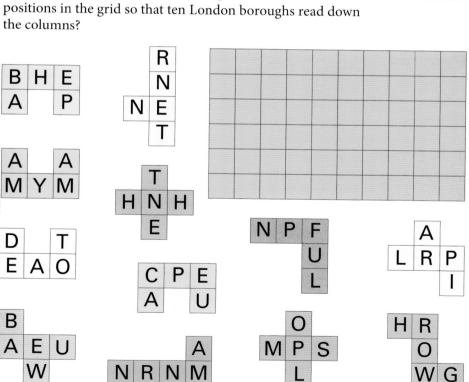

WORKOUT 101

Codewords

If WATER=12345 and TONIC=36789, how quickly can you work out these drinks? You should identify more letters as you go along.

1 3 4 2

2 1 8 7 4

3 9 8 10 4 5

4 11 6 10 2

5 5 4 3 11 8 7 2

Scramble

What geographical terms can be made from each of these sets of scrambled letters?

1 PACE

2 LEAD

3 STEW

4 HORSE

5 RESTED

6 MASTER

7 EPIC COP

8 USE TRAY

9 SWAP CON

10 DRAGSLEEVE

Pyramid

TIME

Each answer except the uses all the letters – usually in a different order – from the previous answer plus one extra letter.

1 First vowel

2 Thank you

3 Took a seat

4 Cures leather

5 Holy patron – England's is George

6 Infusion of camomile leaves or barley water

7 Baltic republic, capital Tallinn

8 Deferential

9 Male singers

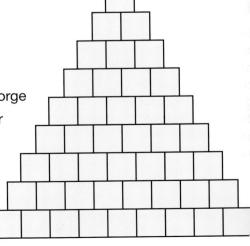

Fitword

TIME

When all of the listed words have been placed correctly in the grid, which one is left over?

3 letters
Ask
Buy
Kin
Koi
Raw
Vow

4 letters
Idea
Yeti

5 letters
Clown
Daily
Dross
Fused
Havoc
Onset

6 letters
Agency
Gargle
Hereby

7 letters
Artwork
~~Basmati~~

8 letters
Biannual
Staffing

Alpha-Beater

TIME

Every letter of the alphabet has been removed from this crossword. How quickly can you put all 26 back? Use the A-Z list to cross off letters as you use them.

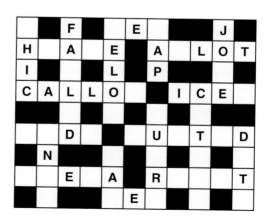

Pathfinder

TIME

Beginning with ANEMONE, and moving up, down, left or right, one letter at a time, can you trace a path of eighteen flowers?

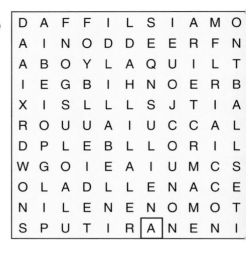

Futoshiki

TIME

Fill the blank squares so that each row and column contains all the numbers 1, 2 and 3. Use the given numbers and the symbols that tell you if the number in the square is larger (>) or smaller (<) than the number next to it.

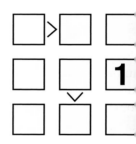

Small Change

TIME

Can you change one letter of each of these words to make five new words with a common theme?

1 MERRY • MUG • JUNE • CANON • TALKER

2 DUNE • THICK • COW • WHEAT • GULP

3 SHOW • FRONT • HAIR • RUIN • SHEET

4 BRAWN • CRAG • CLAY • TINKLE • CACKLE

TIME

Disavowel

Can you complete this puzzle by adding all the vowels?

There are 12 As, 13 Es, 5 Is, 12 Os and 3 Us in the puzzle.

	B					P	L		R		L
R								N		V	
	S	T	R			L		D			S
L		R		D			H		R	D	
	N			D							R
						T	W		N		
R		C		C					G	R	
	S	H	L		R		N				
			D	R				S	T		B
R		N		G						V	
	R		R		S			R	Y		

Sudoku

TIME

Use your powers of reasoning to place numbers in the grid, so that each row, each column and each 3x3 block contains the numbers 1-9.

								5
8	3		7				1	
		2		9			3	
	8			1	3	9	4	7
4								1
9	7	1	6	4			5	
	4			8		1		
	5				9		2	4
7								

Three in One

TIME

The three parts of each clue lead to the same answer word. Can you solve any before you reach the third part?

1 Draft of a proposed law • Beak • Invoice
2 Professorship • Person in charge of a meeting • Seat
3 Prevalent • Piece of land for public use • Vulgar
4 Tolerate • Erode • Have on as clothing
5 Short period • Charm • Name letters of a word in order

Mini Fit

Which one of the listed words won't fit in each of these mini grids?

OUT
TOW
TWO
TUT
WIT

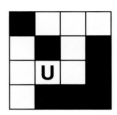

FLU
FLY
FRY
FUR
RYE

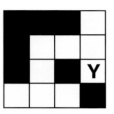

ALLY
LEAD
LILY
LORD
REAL

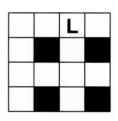

CHIN
CORN
EACH
HAIR
IRON

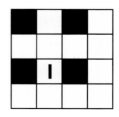

Wordsearch TIME

Hidden in this wordsearch grid ar
fifteen Greek islands.

S	L	C	N	S	P	S	I	C
O	E	E	N	A	X	O	S	C
M	T	P	G	Z	S	N	S	C
A	E	H	S	E	D	O	H	F
S	R	A	A	O	C	K	V	F
E	C	L	P	S	N	Y	E	L
U	T	O	I	A	S	M	Y	F
M	D	N	R	K	R	O	E	C
S	K	I	A	T	H	O	S	L
W	C	A	H	Z	A	T	S	J
I	N	I	R	O	T	N	A	S

Codewords

If BEACH=12345 and
SHORE=65782, how quickly can
you work out these beach words?
You should identify another letter
as you go along.

1 6 2 3

2 4 8 3 1

3 4 7 3 6 9

4 8 2 6 7 8 9

5 1 3 9 5 2 8 6

Mind the Gap

TIME

Can you complete the five words in each set by adding the same three-letter word? For example OUR in HLY, FL, FTH (hourly, flour, fourth), and so on.

MUY PAA DESY HUNG ROUE

DET APEL COME SROW ASAGUS

CTY STER EMPIC WSIT LYMPIC

4 ANM FAR CLOD WEAR APARID

5 CHAI SULA FOOTH IMIENT COMIBLE

Staircase

TIME

When these girls names are correctly fitted in the rows of the grid, another will appear down the diagonal staircase.

AMELIA

CLAIRE

GEORGIA

IMOGEN

KELLY

LILLIAN

PAULINE

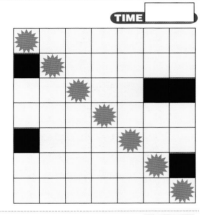

Kakuro

TIME

Simple addition and a bit of logical thinking will solve this one. You must write a digit in each white square so that the digits in each across section add up to the total in the triangle to the left, and the digits in each column add up to the total in the triangle above. 1-9 are the only digits to use and, although you may find a digit repeated in a row, it must not be repeated in the same section. We've solved one section for you.

WORKOUT 107

Arroword

Just follow the arrows to write your answers in the grid. A handful of anagram clues will get you thinking differently.

Angola's continent ▼	World superpower (inits) ▼		CARS (anag) ▼		Keeps happy		Urban horizon	Loud piercing cr
Patties of seafood and potato ►					▼			▼
— Maria, coffee liqueur		Partner in war	Singer Ms Winehouse ►				NEAT (anag)	
►		▼	Frozen water	Person who reigns ►			▼	
Short piece (of video) ►		▼		TIES (anag) ►				
►			Reddish dye used on hair ►					
Bathroom powder	Japanese currency ►			Fabric joint ►				

Vowel Play

Can you replace the missing vowels to complete these dogs?

1	P G	**6**	L R C H R
2	B X R	**7**	S M Y D
3	C R G	**8**	L S T N
4	B G L	**9**	R T R V R
5	C L L	**10**	T R R R

Codewords

If KILO is 1234 and ROMEO is 54674, how quickly can you work out these NATO phonetic alphabet words? You should identify more letters as you go along.

1 6 2 1 7

2 3 2 6 8

3 7 9 10 4

4 11 2 7 5 5 8

5 9 10 8 5 3 2 7

114

Wordsearch

How quickly can you find the seven themed words in each grid?

DIAMONDS

D	Z	Q	H	D	Y	C
B	L	U	X	Y	N	O
M	G	A	R	N	E	T
I	L	R	R	U	S	A
J	A	T	L	E	B	U
N	P	Z	V	X	M	Y
T	O	P	A	Z	O	E

CLUBS

W	P	J	H	R	T	Y
E	G	U	S	R	T	O
R	A	U	O	E	P	X
C	U	U	I	R	D	E
G	P	C	N	L	G	K
E	O	B	A	N	D	Z
S	E	L	C	R	I	C

SPADES

L	M	N	E	S	F	M
F	E	O	O	R	O	J
X	H	V	W	A	R	Q
V	Z	S	O	E	K	W
E	K	A	R	H	R	G
U	I	B	R	S	S	A
T	R	O	W	E	L	H

Letter Sequence

What letter should replace the question mark in these sequences?

1 B, D, H, K, M, Q, ?

2 A, N, C, P, ?, S, J, W

3 E, R, F, ?, G, W, H

4 R, O, Y, G, B, I, ?

5 G, W, V, E, G, E, G, ?

Four by Four

How quickly can you solve this mini crossword?

1	2	3	4
5			
6			
7			

ACROSS
1 Grow boring
5 Opera song
6 Rain heavily
7 Metal fastener

DOWN
1 Footway
2 Zone, region
3 Falsehoods
4 Bedside light

Pairs

Pair off 24 of the listed words to form twelve "double-barreled" words and rearrange the letters of the two words left over to reveal a safety exit.

BACK	GAMMON	ROYAL
BEAN	MANNERS	RUNNER
BIKE	MARINE	SAFE
BIRTH	MARKET	STONE
BLACK	MAT	STRING
CARD	MOUNTAIN	TABLE
DAY	PENNY	VEST
DOOR	POLE	VISITING
FRONT	RECIPE	

Splits

Can you rearrange each of these sets of letter blocks into a word?

1 DE BAR CA RI

2 EN TE UN CIA

3 US ING EN IO

4 ING AT UR FE

5 OU DE HI SLY

Box Wise

Can you place the three-letter groups in the boxes, so that neighbouring boxes always make a six-letter word, like PAR-DON or DON-ATE? We've placed one group to start you off.

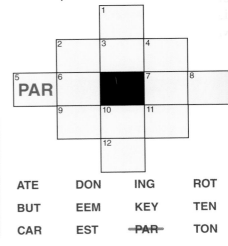

ATE	DON	ING	ROT
BUT	EEM	KEY	TEN
CAR	EST	~~PAR~~	TON

Mini Jigsaw

Fit the pieces in the grid to spell out an item of clothing in each row.

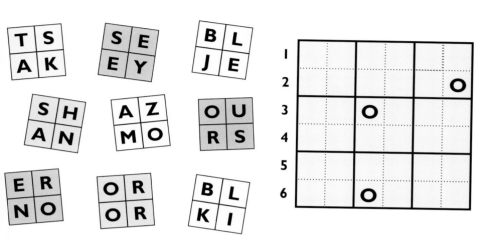

So Complete

Complete each trio of words with a common letter. The five letters will form the answer word. Where there is a choice of completing letter, you must decide which is needed.

DRA_	DA_N	S_AN	
W_ITE	AS_EN	_OIST	
PA_N	SH_FT	L_KE	
MORA_S	CARE_S	CHA_E	
_ING	WIN_	S_IN	

Word Builder

Using the nine letters provided, can you answer these clues? Every answer must include the highlighted letter M. Which type of creature uses all nine letters?

5 Letters
OT song
Baby buggies
Trade downturn
Light-splitting device
Tia ___, coffee-flavoured liqueur
Posts
Dark purple stone fruits

6 Letters
Wall paintings
Liquid part of blood
Spicy sausage
Fundamental, original
Warning sounds

7 Letters
Medieval Japanese feudal warriors
African antelopes

Take Five

The three answers in this mini-crossword read the same across and down. We've clued the three answers, but not in the right order. See how quickly you can solve it.

Auctioneer's hammer

Eagle's claw

Number in an octet

Wild Words

TIME

What well-known phrases and expressions are suggested by these word pictures?

1 KⓣNF̵G

R
O
3 ROADS
D
S

2 111111 other other other other other **other**

4 AcCAUGHTt

Missing Link

TIME

The three words in each clue have a fourth word in common, and that's your answer. For example, the clue "Moon • Navy • Royal" gives the answer BLUE (blue moon, navy blue, royal blue). Write each answer in the grid, and the shaded column will reveal a fruit.

1 Comfort • Shoulder • Stone

2 Cap • Deep • Jerk

3 Free • Half • Lag

4 Log • Open • Rest

5 Dock • Mine • Lady

1				
2				
3				
4				
5				

Elimination

TIME

All but two of the listed words fall into one of the four categories. Put these leftover words together, and what word or phrase do they make?

CATEGORIES Body part anagrams • Green things • Words following OIL (e.g., Seed) • Square numbers

Sixteen	Keen	Lime	Viler	Nine	Emerald
Rig	Grass	Step	Earth	Skin	Jade
Two	Olive	Drum	Twenty-five	Well	
Lose	One	Slick	Café	Four	

WORKOUT 113

Mini Fit

Which one of the listed words won't
fit in each of these mini grids?

DEN
DUE
END
NOD
ODE

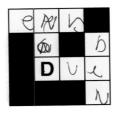

APT
ATE
PAT
SET
SIP

Memory Jog

You have two minutes to study the list of twenty words. Then give yourself
another two minutes to write as many as you can recall on a separate piece
of paper.

UPSTAIRS	OBVIOUSLY	QUALITY	VERIFY	TOOTH
ANOTHER	OAR	RAIN	OUTSIDE	PUPPY
LAMP	ACORN	BLOOD	MOREOVER	STALL
PICTURE	REMINDER	CLIP	COUNT	LEAF

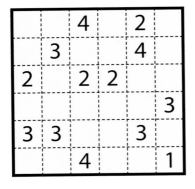

Cell Blocks

Fill the grid by drawing blocks along the
gridlines. Each block must be square or
rectangular and must contain the number
of squares indicated by the digit inside it.
Each block must contain only one digit.

Sudoku

TIME

Place a number in each empty square so that each row, each column and each 2x2 block contains all the numbers from 1-4.

3			2
	4	3	
	3	2	
4			3

	4		3
2		4	

(second grid, corrected)

	4		3
2		4	

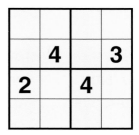

	4		
		2	
		1	
	2		

Add Up

TIME

If the number in each circle is the sum of the two below it, how quickly can you figure out the top number? Try this one in your head, before writing anything down.

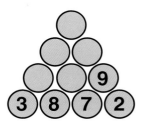

3 8 7 2 — 9

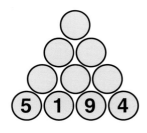

5 1 9 4

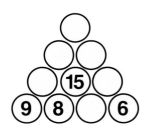

9 8 ( ) 6 — 15

121

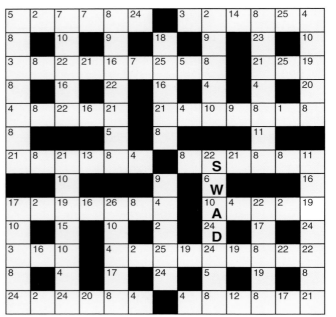

Codeword

Can you crack the code and fill in the crossword grid? Each letter of the alphabet makes at least one appearance in the grid, and is represented by the same number wherever it appears. The four letters we've decoded should help you to identify other letters and words in the grid.

Spot the Sum

In each of these boxes, one of the numbers is the sum of two others. Can you spot the sum?

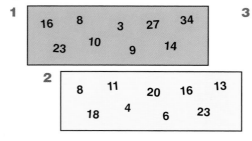

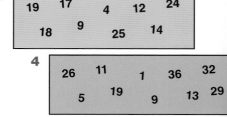

Niners

TIME

Form four nine-letter words using all twelve listed "syllables" (without altering the order of the letters in each "syllble"). Then enter them in the grid in the right order to reveal the sound of a donkey reading down the left-hand column.

AIL	AUT	BLA
CKM	DAY	ISH
LEN	OMA	REP
TER	TON	YES

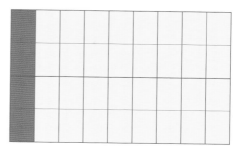

Mane Line

Which numbered photograph has been taken?

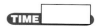
TIME

WORKOUT 117

Mobile Code TIME

If HARRISON is 42774766 on this phone keypad, which famous Georges have the following numbers?

1 2653
2 2566639
3 367629
4 3673626
5 6424235
6 7377273

Logical TIME

How quickly can you figure out what's what?

There are three particularly popular pigs at a local country farm. From the information given below, work out how long each pig has been at the farm (three, four or five years), their favourite activity and which pigpen they sleep in.

Trotter has been at the farm longer than Hambo, whose favourite activity is truffle hunting. The mudbath isn't the activity of choice for Curly, the pig that has spent five years at the farm. The pig that stays in the West pen enjoys football, while the pig in the North pen has spent a year longer at the farm than the pig in the South pen.

Honeycomb TIME

Write the six-letter answers clockwise round their respective cell-numbers, starting at the arrowed cell. On completion, you will find that the unclued answers (10 and 11) will reveal someone of lesser importance – in the strings?

1 Three times over
2 Tame and placid
3 Tended the sick
4 Nearly
5 Delphi's prophetic shrine
6 Sheep's shorn coat
7 Bestow
8 Game bird
9 Dried grape

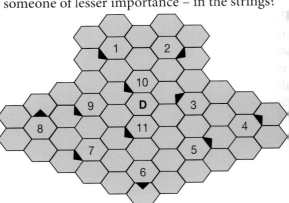

Fitword

TIME

When all of the listed words have been placed correctly in the grid, which one is left over?

3 letters
Luge
Dew
Maim
Ill
~~Rump~~
Inn
Tsar
Used
4 letters
Yoga
Bred
Edgy
7 letters
Know
Firmest
Load
Magical

Slowing
Steered

9 letters
Ascending
Silliness

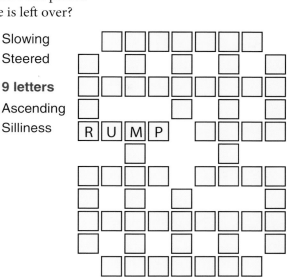

Set Square

TIME

Place one each of the digits 1-9 in the grid to make the sums work. We've put in some of the numbers to start you off. Sums should be solved from left to right, or from top to bottom.

WORKOUT 119

Pathfinder TIME

Beginning with MAORI, and moving up, down, left or right, one letter at a time, can you trace a path of nineteen languages?

D	E	W	S	M	A	Y	N	A	R	E
I	R	U	I	R	O	S	W	M	O	S
S	K	T	I	L	I	H	A	A	N	E
H	I	S	L	A	N	S	H	P	H	C
H	I	H	E	I	D	I	J	A	U	E
D	N	I	C	C	A	N	U	D	R	Z
I	F	L	O	P	P	S	I	A	N	C
E	R	I	H	P	U	I	S	R	H	S
N	C	S	C	T	N	B	S	U	L	I
K	H	H	D	U	J	A	E	L	G	N
A	S	H	M	I	R	I	W	S	H	E

Number Jig TIME

Which one of the listed numbers won't fit in each of these mini grids?

208
284
420
824
842

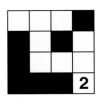

153
397
531
751
915

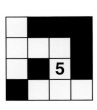

1627
2126
2272
6621
7261

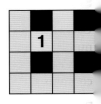

Alpha-Fit TIME

Each of the 26 letters of the alphabet appears once in this crossword.

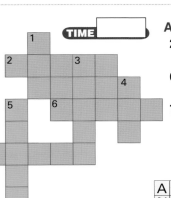

ACROSS
2 Cry of a duck (5)
6 Female fox (5)
7 Norwegian inlets (6)

DOWN
1 Adhesive substance (3)
3 French fries (5)
4 Spider's snare (3)
5 Monetary unit of Poland (5)

A	B	C	D	E	F	G	H	I	J	K	L	M
N	O	P	Q	R	S	T	U	V	W	X	Y	Z

126

Pyramid

Each answer except the first uses all the letters – usually in a different order – from the previous answer plus one extra letter.

1 Food additives number
2 Concerning
3 Keen resentment
4 Old Ireland
5 Coal-face worker
6 Stay
7 Mosque's tower
8 Airport check-in and departure building
9 Outer markings around a tennis court

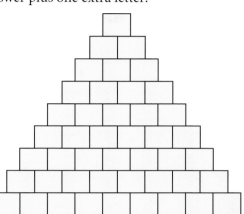

Sudoku

Use your powers of reasoning to place numbers in the grid, so that each row, each column and each 3x3 block contains the numbers 1-9.

	7				9			
	2			9	1	7		
1							8	5
		4		2				1
8		6		5		2		4
3			1		6			
7	9							6
		1	6	3			9	
		3			4			

Staircase

When the seven rivers are correctly placed along the horizontal rows, the letters in the diagonal "staircase" will yield an eighth.

DANUBE
DARLING
GANGES
GARONNE
TRENT
YELLOW
ZAMBEZI

127

WORKOUT 121

Sudoku TIME

Place a number in each empty square so that each row, each column and each 2x2 block contains all the numbers from 1-4.

			3
			1
3			
2			4

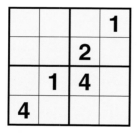

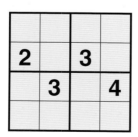

Wordsearch TIME

Hidden in this wordsearch grid are fourteen musical instruments.

C	L	A	R	I	N	E	T	I
O	B	O	E	E	D	G	C	R
B	N	Y	K	N	R	L	U	B
E	A	A	D	O	U	O	A	R
T	C	N	I	H	M	S	T	E
U	A	E	J	P	S	M	R	H
L	N	I	L	O	I	V	U	T
F	Z	N	O	L	W	E	M	I
S	J	N	V	Y	O	P	P	Z
P	R	A	H	X	B	X	E	H
G	U	I	T	A	R	F	T	T

Four by Four TIME

How quickly can you solve this mini crossword?

1	2	3	4
5			
6			
7			

ACROSS
1 Electric cable
5 Biblical garden
6 Soft heavy metal
7 ___ *Army*, classic TV sitcom

DOWN
1 Join (metal) using heat
2 Concept
3 Peruse
4 Terminates

Smart Sums

Try to avoid writing down anything but the final answers to these calculations... no counting on figures allowed either!

1 Lines in a sonnet ÷ days in a week
2 Sides on a hexagon + consonants in MEANDER
3 Sections of an orchestra X syllables in ANEMONE
4 Months in 17 years − wheels on a tandem
5 Number of blackbirds baked in a pie X the number of blind mice

Opposites Attract

Can you sort each set of letter blocks into two words with opposite meanings?

1 AD BRO ED KE LO
2 TH RA SE ER TO TE PA GE
3 IV IC PU PR ATE BL
4 OP IM RE PR COR ER CT

Kakuro

Simple addition and a bit of logical thinking will solve this one. You must write a digit in each white square so that the digits in each across section add up to the total in the triangle to the left, and the digits in each column add up to the total in the triangle above. 1-9 are the only digits to use and, although you may find a digit repeated in a row, it must not be repeated in the same section. We've solved one section for you.

			8	20	6	23		12	16
		13					17		
	3	4					6		
45									
4	1	3	19						

WORKOUT 123

Arroword

Just follow the arrows to write your answers in the grid. A handful of anagram clues will get you thinking differently.

Cut in two ▼		Make a choice ▼		Part of a guitar's fingerboard ▼		Cavort, gambol ▼		Meal period	LATENT (anag)
Flawed ▶						▼			▼
Affirmative reply		Pig food		Division of geological time				NOVA (anag)	
▶			▼	Right, fitting	Final amount ▶		▼		
Scallop ▶			▼			Reside ▶			
				— Pegg, Hot Fuzz star ▶					
POTS (anag)	Go to next page (inits) ▶			US monetary unit ▶					

Splits

Can you rearrange each of these sets of letter blocks into a word?

1 IS ES TS SAY

2 OF RE FI PRO

3 SC AR HOL LY

4 UND RO NA RU

5 RI DEX TY TE

Logical

Try solving this little logical problem in your head before putting pen to paper.

Three friends each won a medal at their school's sports day. If Chuck got silver, but not in the discus, and Sanjeev's long jump got him a higher placing than the contestant in the 100m, which event did Russell take part in, and where did he come?

Cake Bake

Which two pictures are identical?

Two of a Kind

Can you sort each set of letter blocks into two words with the same meaning?

1 SO LE MP TE LU AB TE CO

2 CO MAG TE NA ON TY

3 MI NE ST EN TY SS OR VA

4 PER CO NT TA NE MA NS NT

5 OR CH ON VI PI CT AM

Staircase

When these furniture items are correctly fitted in the rows of the grid, another such item will appear down the diagonal staircase.

BENCH
CRADLE
DIVAN
ROCKER
TABLE
TALLBOY
WHATNOT

WORKOUT 125

Fare's Fair

Find two words of the same sound but different spelling to satisfy each two-element clue, then decide which of the pair goes where in the grid to discover a spice, reading down the arrowed column.

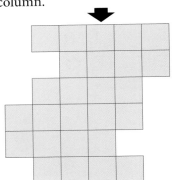

Rule in wet weather

Equitable cost of a journey

Occasion for a herb

Lazy false god

Of sound mind at the river

Correct ceremonial procedure

Memory Jog

Give yourself two minutes to memorise this list of thirty words. How many of them can you recall on a separate piece of paper in another two minutes?

BELLOW	ALTOGETHER
WHITHER	APPLE
FROND	BRACKET
GUIDE	FLASHY
HATSTAND	STEERING
DILIGENTLY	PERSEVERANCE
ROCK	DESPOND
SCREEN	PENCIL
DISCO	FASHION
TYPE	GREETING
CLATTER	PERSIST
STEW	SLANG
QUESTIONNAIRE	RAFFLE
PLAYHOUSE	CREEPY
WOBBLY	
SINCE	

Futoshiki

Fill the blank squares so that each row and column contains all the numbers 1, 2 and 3. Use the given numbers and the symbols that tell you if the number in the square is larger (>) or smaller (<) than the number next to it.

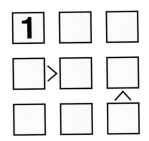

Mini Jigsaw

Fit the pieces in the grid to spell out a dessert in each row.

TIME

| E | T | | T | R | | S | U |
| S | E | | Y | O | | G | A |

| L | E | | N | D | | R | B |
| R | T | | T | E | | U | S |

| I | F | | S | O | | A | E |
| G | U | | M | O | | A | U |

			E
1			
2			
3			E
4			
5			
6		E	

Killer Sudoku

TIME

The normal rules of Sudoku apply. Place a digit from 1-9 in each empty square so that each row, column and 3x3 block contains all the digits from 1-9. In addition, the digits in each inner shape (marked by dots) must add up to the number in the top corner of that box. No digit can be repeated within an inner shape.

Killer Sudoku grid clues: 26, 10, 19, 16, 13, 7, 7, 22, 14, 8, 10, 14, 16, 12, 13, 12, 8, 17, 16, 12, 6, 9, 4, 10, 20, 22, 12, 5, 13, 12, 8, 12

Word Builder

Using the nine letters provided, can you answer these clues? Every answer must include the highlighted letter C. Which form of betterment uses all nine letters?

5 Letters
Caper
Move to music
Sharp
Make into law
Vast sea
Gin accompaniment
Small narrow boat

6 Letters
Big-billed bird
Director's cry
Church official
Persuade, talk into
Petrol ingredient

7 Letters
Espied
Added up
Tube for carrying fluid

9 Letters
Warned
Sold to the highest bidder

Wordsearch

How quickly can you find the seven themed words in each grid?

ROYAL

I	S	N	G	R	P	S
D	I	T	C	N	R	M
Q	U	E	E	N	I	O
J	Q	K	O	K	N	K
V	R	R	E	Q	C	F
Y	A	L	R	A	E	H
B	M	B	U	D	P	X

OPERA

O	L	L	E	T	O	H
N	N	C	X	T	T	T
O	E	Z	D	E	O	F
R	M	U	B	S	A	A
M	R	C	C	K	D	U
A	A	A	G	M	I	S
M	C	I	J	H	A	T

HOUSE

C	O	O	L	G	I	I
N	O	I	S	N	A	M
T	M	T	L	S	H	E
Y	A	W	T	C	N	S
V	I	L	L	A	X	A
O	E	J	F	D	G	K
B	E	D	S	I	T	E

Niners

TIME

Form four nine-letter words using all twelve listed "syllables" (without altering the order of the letters in each "syllable"). Then enter them in the grid in the right order to reveal a European capital city reading down the left-hand column.

AGE	CEM	EAS
EAT	ECT	HAN
MIN	OLL	ORP
RDS	REC	TWA

Set Square

TIME

Place one each of the digits 1-9 in the grid to make the sums work. We've put in some of the numbers to start you off. Sums should be solved from left to right, or from top to bottom.

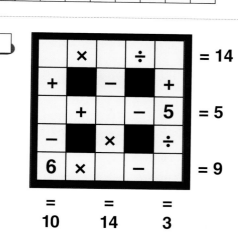

Elimination

TIME

All but two of the listed words fall into one of the four categories. Put these leftover words together, and what phrase do they make?

CATEGORIES Santa's reindeer • Words preceding BALL (e.g., foot) • Egg-laying creatures • Dances

Hand	Boy	Bee	Dasher	Tango	Samba
Goose	Vixen	Screw	Odd	Dancer	Punch
Foxtrot	Pin	Jive	Cupid	Principal	
Comet	Waltz	Turtle	Platypus	Salmon	

135

WORKOUT 129

Wordsearch

TIME

How quickly can you find the five themed words in each grid?

BIG ___

U	M	B	A	N	G	B
X	D	O	N	T	R	Z
Y	I	Q	U	O	T	G
K	P	W	T	T	O	P
J	P	H	L	S	H	B
R	E	F	M	E	S	C
R	R	I	V	D	O	H

SMALL ___

E	R	A	T	X	J	F
G	H	E	C	I	O	Z
N	R	E	E	R	M	V
A	O	W	T	B	I	E
H	L	U	F	R	Y	Q
C	N	K	Y	S	T	B
E	M	P	D	F	N	U

Pairs

TIME

Pair off 24 of the listed words to form twelve "double-barreled" words and rearrange the letters of the two words left over to reveal a condiment

ARM	FIELD	SCARLET	CENTER	LINE	WINDOW	EAGLE
FEVER	REST	BREAK	GERM	VALIANT	DOWN	OUT
PITCH	BOW	GARDEN	TIE	CRICKET	NECK	
BORDER	FRENCH	SPREAD	CHAIR	MARKET	WOMAN	

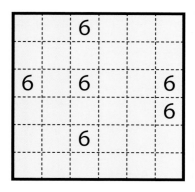

Cell Blocks

TIME

Fill the grid by drawing blocks along the gridlines. Each block must be square or rectangular and must contain the number of squares indicated by the digit inside it. Each block must contain only one digit.

136

Sudoku   TIME

Place a number in each empty square so that each row, each column and each 2x2 block contains all the numbers from 1-4.

1			2
	2	4	
	1	2	
2			4

4			2
	2	1	
	4	2	
2			1

4			3
	3	4	
	1	3	
3			1

Add Up   TIME

If the number in each circle is the sum of the two below it, how quickly can you figure out the top number? Try this one in your head, before writing anything down.

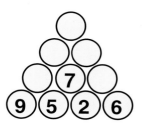

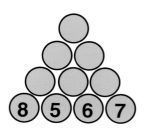

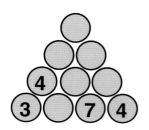

Codeword

TIME [ ]

Can you crack the code and fill in the crossword grid? Each letter of the alphabet makes at least one appearance in the grid, and is represented by the same number wherever it appears. The four letters we've decoded should help you to identify other letters and words in the grid.

	7		6		11				9		21	
3	25	12	22	20	16	15		4	6	21	12	22
	10		16		17		23		25		22	
15	22	13	17		4	6	26	15	8	25	6	4
		17		16		15		22		17		
25	17	17	26	6	25(R)	15(A)	2(N)	22(C)		13	7	14
	5		22		1		18		4		21	
9	26	1		16	15	19	26	6	16	25	18	22
	16		17		21		25		17			
23	6	21	23	21	17	25	20		6	25	19	18
	11		21		22		16		26		16	
6	22	11	16	24		17	18	26	23	22	19	14
	4		20			14		18		22		

A̶ B C̶ D E F G H I J K L M N̶ O P Q R̶ S T U V W X Y Z

1	2 C	3	4	5	6 R	7	8	9	10	11	12	13
14	15 N	16	17	18	19	20	21	22	23	24	25 A	26

Masyu

TIME [ ]

For this Japanese logic puzzle, you must draw a line around the grid that passes through ALL the black and white dots before joining up with itself to make a continuous loop. Your line can pass through or turn left or right in empty squares, but there are rules for squares containing dots. Your line cannot cross over itself, branch off, or go through the same square twice.

Rules for dots

Black Dot: Your line must turn left or right in these boxes, and pass straight through the next and previous boxes.

White Dot: Your line must travel straight through the box, and it must turn left or right in the next box and/or the previous box.

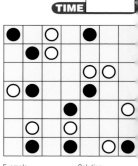

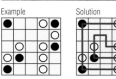

Example   Solution

Splits

Can you rearrange each of these sets of letter blocks into a word?

1 HE PER RY IP   4 NAG ME IE ER
2 RE CH CA ILD   5 RED AT WE HE
3 NEE TI MU RS

Baby Face

Which numbered photograph has been taken?

Number Sequence

What number should replace the question mark in these sequences?

1 1, 5, 14, 30, 55, ?

2 1, 9, 7, 16, 13, 23, 19, ?

3 7, 8, 5, 5, 3, 4, 4, ?

4 ...6, 4, 8, 14, 18, 26, 40, ?

5 ...10, 14, 22, 38, ?, 134

Initials

If ITHOTN (Oscar-winning film) is *IN THE HEAT OF THE NIGHT*, what do these initials represent?

1 KK (Film monster)

2 OAL (Nursery school song)

3 TLD (Scenic area)

4 TLTOP (World landmark)

5 JATATD (Musical)

Pyramid

Each answer except the first uses all the letters – usually in a different order – from the previous answer plus one extra letter.

1 Spain's vehicle registration letter

2 Musical note

3 Game, ___ and match

4 Remainder

5 Guide

6 Difficult question

7 (Of leaves) having a sawlike edge

8 Move across a mountain face

9 Reaper

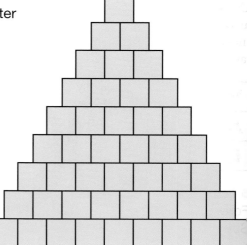

Fitword

TIME

When all of the listed words have been placed correctly in the grid, which one is left over?

3 letters
Bad
But
Ebb
Its
Sob
Tea

4 letters
Also
Rode

Room
Snob
Stay
Yips

5 letters
Basil
Catty
Cocoa
Farce
Gusto

Mogul
~~Rogue~~
Sides
Tasty

7 letters
Cramped
Tinting

Word Builder

TIME

Using the nine letters provided, can you answer these clues? Every answer must include the highlighted letter N. Which law enforcer uses all nine letters?

5 Letters
Foreign
Spy

Belly-button
Heavenly creature
Innocent
Point of view

6 Letters
Indigenous
Set fire to
Kind

Ask to come
Knot (of hair, e.g.,)
Involve

7 Letters
Departing
Classic (of cars, e.g.,)
Shadowing
Masking

8 Letters
Watchful
Cleaning and parking cars

WORKOUT 135

Pathfinder TIME

Beginning with FARFALLE, and moving up, down, left or right, one letter at a time, can you trace a path of fifteen types of pasta?

L	I	E	N	G	A	S	R	A	M	I
L	R	R	R	E	R	A	O	C	A	L
E	A	A	O	G	I	L	N	I	I	L
M	V	D	T	A	E	S	O	N	S	U
E	I	I	A	T	L	D	O	A	L	F
G	O	L	I	O	F	A	R	F	L	E
I	L	H	G	N	L	I	E	L	H	I
E	L	E	A	I	G	A	T	L	C	G
C	I	T	P	T	A	I	U	E	N	L
R	M	T	S	S	A	N	G	C	O	I
E	V	I	A	T	P	E	N	I	L	E

Number Jig TIME

Which one of the listed numbers won't fit in each of these mini grids?

121
125
250
510
515

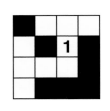

293
324
439
492
942

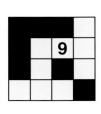

3689
3739
6793
6837
9638

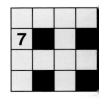

TIME

Leaf Alone

Can you spot the nine differences between these pictures?

Spot the Sum

In each of these boxes, one of the numbers is the sum of two others. Can you spot the sum?

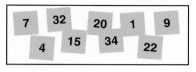

3

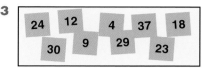

2

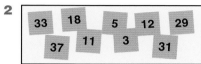

4

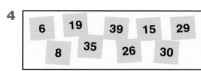

Sudoku

Use your powers of reasoning to place numbers in the grid, so that each row, each column and each 3x3 block contains the numbers 1-9.

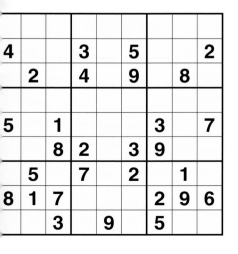

Scramble

The names of which star constellations can be made from each of these sets of scrambled letters? Some will be much more familiar than others!

1 OLE

2 ARISE

3 IN ROO

4 OH GULP

5 SPICES

6 EAGER BRAT (5,4)

7 DEAD ROMAN

8 CAIRN CROP

Six Pack

Can you place digits in the empty triangles, so that the numbers in each hexagon add up to 25? Only single digits between 1 and 9 can be used, and no two numbers in any hexagon may be the same.

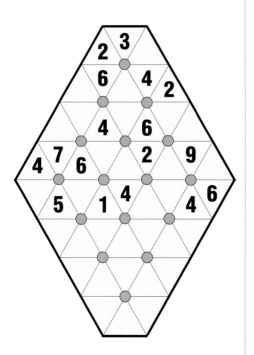

Wordsearch **TIME**

Hidden in this wordsearch grid are fifteen States.

H	A	W	A	I	I	O	G	M
F	A	F	L	O	R	I	D	A
X	I	R	W	U	A	H	M	V
O	L	A	I	K	R	O	A	E
D	H	D	S	Z	N	J	I	R
A	N	A	T	N	O	M	N	M
E	L	V	D	T	G	N	E	O
A	B	E	T	I	E	O	A	N
N	Q	N	S	W	R	X	C	T
U	T	A	H	K	O	Z	A	A
K	R	O	Y	W	E	N	P	S

Smart Sums **TIME**

Try to avoid writing down anything but the final answers to these calculations…

1 One gross – ounces in 7lbs

2 Days in a leap year – hours in 9 days

3 Suits in a pack of cards x maximum number of spots on a domino

4 Consonants in MAGNANIMOUS + total number of dots on a die

5 Gallons made up by 72 pints x reputed number of lives a cat has

Copycats

Choose the answer that best copies the pattern.

 TIME

WRITE is to PEN as PLAY is to: Sty • Clarinet • Stage • Theatre • Fool

DOVE is to COTE as HARE is to: Gape • Have • Farm • Lair • Holt

PUMA is to AMERICA as TIGER is to: Europe • France • Asia • Korea • Africa

WATER is to LIQUID as OXYGEN is to: Vapor • Steam • Gas • Breath • Air

Memory Jog

Spend two minutes memorising this list of twenty words, then see how many of them you can recall on a separate piece of paper.

WIN	OPEN	BRIGHTNESS	TYRE	RANK
PEARL	THINK	HANDLE	OWL	CRATER
GONG	LOUDLY	RADIO	CHAIN	
BREAKING	MOVEMENT	TICKER		
SPEND	FUME	RACKETEER		

Kakuro

TIME

Simple addition and a bit of logical thinking will solve this one. You must write a digit in each white square so that the digits in each across section add up to the total in the triangle to the left, and the digits in each column add up to the total in the triangle above. 1-9 are the only digits to use and, although you may find a digit repeated in a row, it must not be repeated in the same section. We've solved one section for you.

Kakuro grid — column clues: 22, 16, 15, 4, 8, 7. Row clues: 16\16, 4, 4\4 with solved cells 1 and 3; 45; 14, 16, 6. Solved section shows values 1 and 3.

145

Arroword

Just follow the arrows to write your answers in the grid. A handful of anagram clues will get you thinking differently.

Religious writings	Heron-like bird	Bed dress	▼	Commercial channel (inits) ▼	▼	Pop-band follower ▼	▼	SKA (anag)	▼
▶	▼								
Public washing place		Slang word for 'clothing'	Put in the mail		List of actors		Confide in		
▶		▼	▼	Slice or trim ▶	▼		▼		Rob ___ Scottish her
Jotting sheets ▶									▼
▶				SOIL (anag) ▶					
BINGE (anag)	In a calm controlled way ▶								

Vowel Play

Can you replace the missing vowels to complete the names of these herbs and spices?

1 B Y
2 M C
3 M N T
4 S G
5 N S

6 B R G
7 N S D
8 R G N
9 R S M R Y
10 T R M R C

Small Change

Can you change one letter of each of these words to make five new words with a common theme?

1 HALF • LEFT • CLAMBER • QUITE • COLLAR
2 BLOOD • STALE • METAL • LOAF • SEND
3 SORE • TONE • LOGGER • DOWER • BAILED
4 HEATING • COUCH • RIGHT • WASTE • SMALL
5 JOB • BLESS • GLUE • CAPTURE • EXALTATION

Fix Six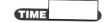

The six animals listed will fit into this pattern of six adjoining hexagons. All are entered clockwise from a triangle to be discovered.
Adjoining triangles always contain the same letter. The K gives you a start.

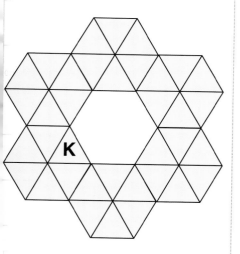

BADGER	GERBIL
COUGAR	OCELOT
FERRET	SALUKI

Mobile Code TIME

If ODD is 633 on this phone keypad, what mathematical terms have the following numbers?

1 786
2 6326
3 7668
4 82583
5 628749

Four by Four

How quickly can you solve this mini crossword?

1	2	3	4
5			
6			
7			

ACROSS
1 Reserve
5 Peak, apex
6 Curds and ___, Miss Muffet's lunch
7 Part of the eye

DOWN
1 Yell
2 Darts players' line
3 Forewarning
4 Typewriter levers

147

Set Square

TIME

Place one each of the digits 1-9 in the grid to make the sums work. We've put in some of the numbers to start you off. Sums should be solved from left to right, or from top to bottom.

	−		×		= 36
−	■	×	■	÷	
1	×		÷		= 2
×	■	÷	■	+	
	×	2	−		= 3

=	=	=
35	12	10

Take Five

TIME

The three answers in this mini-crossword read the same across and down. We've clued the three answers, but not in the right order. See how quickly you can solve it.

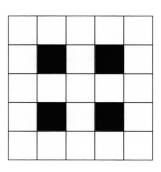

Well done!

Black wood

Item of furniture

Mind the Gap

TIME

Can you place a well-known three-letter word in the spaces of each row to complete the seven-letter word? Do it correctly, and the shaded letters should spell out something associated with Advent.

S	E				E	D
D	E				N	T
D	E	P				E
T	R	O				R
S				G	L	E
M	A				N	S
H	O				R	S
R	E				O	F

Mini Jigsaw

TIME

Fit the pieces in the grid to spell out something found in the kitchen in each row.

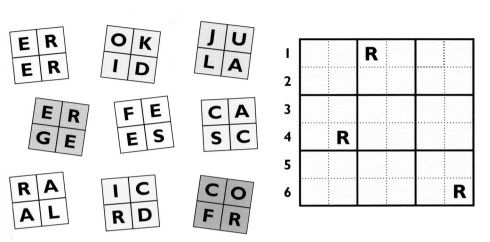

Killer Sudoku

TIME

The normal rules of Sudoku apply. Place a digit from 1-9 in each empty square so that each row, column and 3x3 block contains all the digits from 1-9. In addition, the digits in each inner shape (marked by dots) must add up to the number in the top corner of that box. No digit can be repeated within an inner shape.

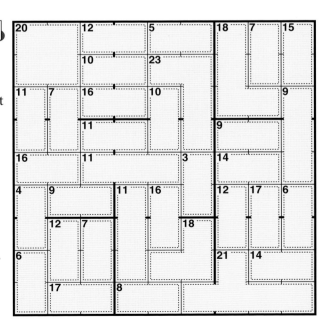

Mini Fit

Which one of the listed words won't fit in each of these mini grids?

AWN
FUN
IDE
USE
WIN

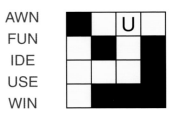

APT
CAP
COW
LAP
OWL

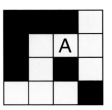

BEST
CART
CUBE
RUSH
WASH

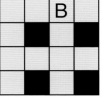

APSE
GLUE
KNEE
OPAL
SPIN

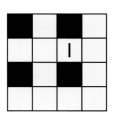

Dominoes

Solve the clues then write the six-letter answers into the dominoes. You must work out whether each word fits in clockwise or anticlockwise, so that the connecting letters of the dominoes all match up.

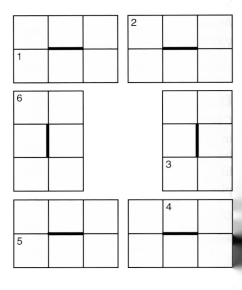

1 Spanish rice dish with shellfish, chicken and vegetables

2 Chinese edible fruit with a whitish juicy pulp

3 Kidney-shaped nut

4 A blackcurrant cordial

5 Dried grape

6 Italian grilled sandwich

Step Riddle

TIME ☐

Can you solve the riddle in five easy steps?

To begin with, I am green fruits, and am found upon a tree. __ __ __ __ __
When you change my first I develop into a daily. __ __ __ __ __
Change a second and you'll find you can still read lots of me. __ __ __ __ __
Alter my third and sound qualities appear. __ __ __ __ __
Swap a fourth letter and I'm useful for curling hair. __ __ __ __ __
At the last, change my last and an island you'll see. __ __ __ __ __
What was I, what did I change into and what did I turn out to be?

Box Wise

TIME ☐

Can you place the three-letter groups in the boxes, so that neighbouring boxes always make a six-letter word, like PAR-DON or DON-ATE? We've placed one group to start you off.

1			
2	3	4 **DER**	
5	6	■	7	8
9	10	11	
	12		

DEN   GAR   MAL   STO
DER   ICE   RAP   TAL
ENT   LET   RED   WAR

Soundalikes

TIME ☐

Can you complete each of these sentences with two words that sound alike, but are spelled differently?

1 The ___ around Elizabeth I's neck was too ___ for the royal skin.
2 The ___ takeaway we have is Chinese, particularly chow ___.
3 Old Mother Hubbard ___ a large pot of tea for her ever-increasing ___ of children.
4 There's no need to ___ about the quality of ___ if it's from a French vineyard.

WORKOUT 145

Wordsearch

How quickly can you find the five themed words in each grid?

BREAD

B	H	L	E	G	A	B
F	L	B	L	T	L	N
A	C	O	T	O	A	S
O	Q	I	O	K	R	R
L	P	W	U	M	F	P
X	J	G	Z	M	E	O
I	E	D	V	Y	T	R

BUTTER

C	R	E	A	M	Y	O
Y	H	Q	K	O	R	X
E	C	E	G	L	F	T
H	D	U	E	H	I	Z
W	R	K	N	S	M	M
T	W	P	G	V	E	I
J	A	Y	U	B	E	L

Splits

How quickly can you find the five themed words in each grid?

Can you rearrange each of these sets of letter blocks into a word?

1 ER PRE NT SE   4 RAP HY GE OG

2 IN CE POR LA   5 NI STO MA FE

3 DER RI AN CO

Cell Blocks

Fill the grid by drawing blocks along the gridlines. Each block must be square or rectangular and must contain the number of squares indicated by the digit inside it. Each block must contain only one digit.

	3				3
	3			2	
3			3		
	4			2	
3					
	3		3		4

Sudoku `TIME`

Place a number in each empty square so that each row, each column and each 2x2 block contains all the numbers from 1-4.

4	3	1	2
2	4	3	1

4			1
	1	4	
	2	1	
1			2

	4	1	
1			3
4			1
	1	3	

Add Up `TIME`

If the number in each circle is the sum of the two below it, how quickly can you figure out the top number? Try this one in your head, before writing anything down.

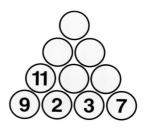

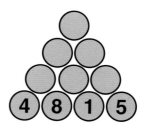

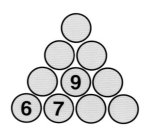

Codeword

Can you crack the code and fill in the crossword grid? Each letter of the alphabet makes at least one appearance in the grid, and is represented by the same number wherever it appears. The four letters we've decoded should help you to identify other letters and words in the grid.

TIME

Grid (across rows):

3		2		22		13		16		4		2
6	13	9 (G)	1	13	9	9	19	1		19	21	19
9 (N)		3		24		23		19		5		14
18 (O)	23	10	3	24	11	20		19	8	13	25	19
1 (R)			3		13				19			25
19	20	16		9	3	6	15	10	24	11	23	
		20		24				19		10		
	16	18	18	10	21	19	11	1		15	18	25
11		13				9		1				3
4	11	9	12	18		6	20	11	17	3	9	6
18		24		11		11		23		10		19
26	3	19		22	18	6	6	3	9	19	22	22
19		25		10		19		9		7		10

A B C D E F G̸ H I J K L M N̸ O̸ P Q R̸ S T U V W X Y Z

| 1 R | 2 | 3 | 4 | 5 | 6 G | 7 | 8 | 9 N | 10 | 11 | 12 | 13 |
| 14 | 15 | 16 | 17 | 18 O | 19 | 20 | 21 | 22 | 23 | 24 | 25 | 26 |

Three in One

TIME

The three parts of each clue lead to the same answer word. Can you solve any before you reach the third part?

1 Instance • Lawsuit • Protective container

2 Enclosure • Write • Female swan

3 Shoemaker's item • Endure • Final

4 Hard stone • Gas or liquid from a nozzle • Airplane

5 Detain • Wrestling move • Ship's cargo store

Memory Jog

Spend two minutes memorising this list of twenty words, then see how many of them you can recall on a separate piece of paper in another two minutes.

AFTERNOON	TOMFOOLERY	CHORTLE	BUTTERFLY
PHYSICS	STATUE	CRACKER	DRAMATIC
OCTOBER	REALISING	WALLPAPER	CAUTION
RAIN	GRAVEL	SILENTLY	EXHAUSTIVE
TEA	SPLATTER	CASCADE	TRAINER

Shape Up

Can you arrange these five-letter shapes into their correct positions in the grid so that five hats and five shoes read down the columns?

TIME

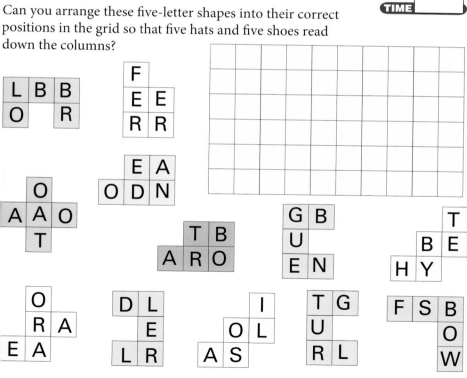

Futoshiki TIME

Fill the blank squares so that each row and column contains all the numbers 1, 2, 3 and 4. Use the given numbers and the symbols that tell you if the number in the square is larger (>) or smaller (<) than the number next to it.

1			>	
			3
	^	^2	

Codewords TIME

If RICE=1234 and SNAP=5678, how quickly can you work out these food words? You should identify one more letter as you go along.

1 8 4 7

2 3 9 1 6

3 3 7 8 4 1

4 3 1 2 5 8

5 5 3 9 6 4

Town to Town TIME

Can you travel from Dalston to West Ham by removing or adding one letter at each stage from the definitions below, which are consequent anagrams?

	D	A	L	S	T	O	N

1 Claws of birds of prey **1**

2 Singing voices **2**

3 Final **3**

4 Posed **4**

5 Afternoon meals **5**

6 Detests **6**

7 London's river **7**

W	E	S	T	H	A	M

Fitword

When all of the listed words have been placed correctly in the grid, which one is left over?

TIME

3 letters		7 letters
Iota		Emperor
Gig	Lobe	Tearing
Tut	Lurk	Tipping

4 letters	5 letters	
Asti	~~Ashen~~	9 letters
Body	Expat	Beseeched
Fray	Noted	Sarcastic
Garb	Rosti	Superstar
Idly		

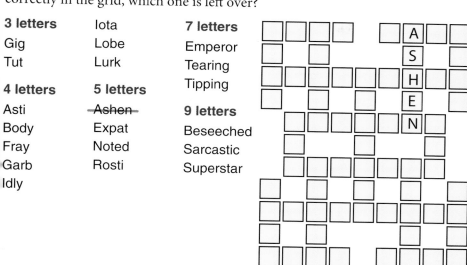

Spot the Sum

TIME

In each of these boxes, one of the numbers is the sum of two others. Can you spot the sum?

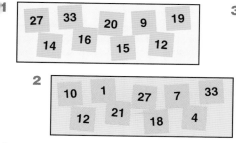

1

27 33 20 9 19
14 16 15 12

2

10 1 27 7 33
12 21 18 4

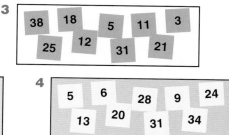

3

38 18 5 11 3
25 12 31 21

4

5 6 28 9 24
13 20 31 34

157

Pathfinder

Beginning with SUSPECT, and moving up, down, left or right, one letter at a time, can you trace a path of seventeen Cluedo words?

D	G	N	I	P	D	A	E	L	R	E
I	N	I	P	N	I	T	D	A	G	G
N	I	O	M	N	U	O	R	M	U	L
G	R	O	W	O	D	P	E	S	S	P
O	P	A	E	H	W	E	F	O	O	R
N	U	D	D	R	O	M	P	R	T	R
S	T	Y	C	A	O	R	U	S	C	E
N	E	R	H	A	L	L	S	P	E	V
N	A	O	V	L	A	B	I	L	R	E
S	P	L	E	L	B	R	E	N	E	N
R	E	V	R	Y	R	A	E	R	G	D

Add Up

If the number in each circle is the sum of the two below it, how quickly can you figure out the top number? Try this one in your head, before writing anything down

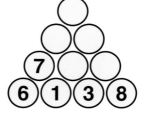

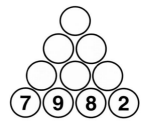

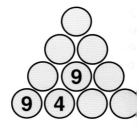

In and Out

Without changing the order of the letters, add or remove one letter each time to leave a (different) new complete word and put the added or removed letters in their respective boxes to find a sales outlet reading down the boxes.

DANE		ROUSE	
NICHE		PLEA	
GLEN		SHOUT	
CLAM		SPIES	
VINE		WEAVE	

Complete Works

Complete each trio of words with a common letter. The five letters will form the answer word. Where there is a choice of completing letter, you must decide which is needed.

TIME

RIC_	S_AM	BAS_
SHE_R	L_VER	_MBER
DRI_E	ALI_E	A_ERT
STR_P	ST_UT	CH_IR
PRI_E	_LICK	_HEAT

Sudoku
TIME

Use your powers of reasoning to place numbers in the grid, so that each row, each column and each 3x3 block contains the numbers 1-9.

				5	4			
	9	6					2	1
	2		1		6			
9	3	1		8		7	6	
4	2	5		7		8	3	
	3		9		5			
	8	4				1	7	
			6	7				

Four by Four
TIME

How quickly can you solve this mini crossword?

¹	²	³	⁴
⁵			
⁶			
⁷			

ACROSS
1 Farm animals
5 Aid illegally
6 Marine flatfish
7 Be of assistance

DOWN
1 Spending money
2 Twin-reeded woodwind instrument
3 Water source
4 Pace

159

Word Builder

Using the nine letters provided, can you answer these clues? Every answer must include the highlighted letter F. Which enthralling word uses all nine letters?

C	A	N
E	**F**	T
S	I	A

5 Letters
Banquet
Exploits, deeds
Small restaurants
Sham attack
Truths
Swoon

6 Letters
Spanish carnival
Do up
Best
Betrothed man
Overrun (with vermin)
Sides of a gem

8 Letters
Most la-di-dah
Avid supporters

Wordsearch TIME

Hidden in this wordsearch grid are fifteen Indian dishes.

A	K	A	S	N	A	H	D	V
D	I	O	B	A	L	T	I	A
N	J	H	R	Z	B	N	M	K
A	C	A	T	M	D	R	A	K
S	N	F	L	A	A	V	D	I
A	D	U	L	F	P	H	R	T
P	Q	O	H	C	R	L	A	W
I	O	A	U	B	A	E	S	L
B	I	R	Y	A	N	I	Z	X
U	R	J	H	E	C	I	R	I
Y	M	P	K	E	E	M	A	N

Splits

Can you rearrange each of these sets of letter blocks into a word?

1 MAN DE NG DI

2 ES ING FR IN

3 GE VE DI STI

4 TA CRE RY SE

5 NE PLE IM CR

Sudoku

TIME

Place a number in each empty square so that each row, each column and each 2x2 block contains all the numbers from 1-4.

	3	4	
4			3
1			4
	4	1	

3			1
	1	2	
	3	1	
1			2

2			4
	3	2	
	2	4	
3			2

Wild Words

TIME

What well-known phrases and expressions are suggested by these word pictures?

1

2

5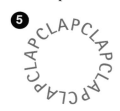

3

4

Kakuro

TIME

Simple addition and a bit of logical thinking will solve this one. You must write a digit in each white square so that the digits in each across section add up to the total in the triangle to the left, and the digits in each column add up to the total in the triangle above. 1-9 are the only digits to use and, although you may find a digit repeated in a row, it must not be repeated in the same section. We've solved one section for you.

(Kakuro grid with clues: across/down totals 8, 4, 15, 16, 22, 13; 4, 16, 16; 4, 7, 16; 45; 6, 1, 5, 4, 14)

WORKOUT 155

Arroword

TIME

Just follow the arrows to write your answers in the grid. A handful of anagram clues will get you thinking differently.

Old superpower (inits) ▼		Koala's habitat (3,4) ▼		Person of Hebrew origin ▼		Beirut's country ▼		Poisonous snake ▼	
►									
Cleverness, shrewdness		Did an impression of		HEAR (anag)		Deep mud		_Sampras, tennis great	
►			▼		▼	AMP (anag) ►	▼		▼ Low in spirits ▼
Fury	Nutty chocolates ►								
►					Duty system ►				
Support vocally	Intensified ►								

Initials

TIME

If ITHOTN (Oscar-winning film) is *IN THE HEAT OF THE NIGHT*, what do these initials represent?

1 ACGAS (Novel and TV series)

2 PO (Chip flavor)

3 SHADW (Fictional detective pair)

4 MHWGO (No.1 hit and film theme)

5 AWTEW (Proverb and play)

Vowel Play

TIME

Can you replace the missing vowels to complete these Christmas words?

1 N L   **6** G R T T

2 C R L   **7** L F

3 R N D R   **8** S N T

4 B B L   **9** W R T H

5 T R   **10** W N C S L

Odd One Out

Which one of these pictures is the odd one out?

Scramble

Which mountains and volcanoes can be forged from each of these sets of scrambled letters?

1 NEAT
2 I, A SIN?
3 NODS NOW
4 SEER VET
5 MY NICKEL
6 THREAT NORM
7 ARK AT OAK
8 MINK OIL AJAR

Four by Four

How quickly can you solve this mini crossword?

1	2	3	4
5			
6			
7			

ACROSS
1 Decorative ribbons
5 Egg-shaped
6 Pool, lake
7 Reared

DOWN
1 Military shell
2 Above
3 Pottery goods
4 Snow vehicle

Number Jig

All but one of these numbers will fit in the grid. How quickly can you get the numbers placed, and which is left over?

3 Digits	4 Digits	7783	41363
344	1252	~~8458~~	52475
446	1325	8580	57206
552	2365	9114	72381
736	2924		88704
810	3130	**5 Digits**	
861	3823	15104	**7 Digits**
868	3884	38271	3758014
932	5743	39265	7884357
	7064		

Mind the Gap

Can you complete the five words in each set by adding the same three-letter word? For example OUR in HLY, FL, FTH (hourly, flour, fourth), and so on.

1 ENTE HOODK PERIKLE RED SAG

2 DEMATION LENIST MH PEL SASM

3 AGE CAUAY ELHERE PRAIORTHY ROOOD

4 BUDS FIDED GADRY MANOUT VEABLE

5 ELES IILITY OBS RUOUT WANE

Missing Link

The three words in each clue have a fourth word in common, and that's your answer. For example, the clue "Moon • Navy • Royal" gives the answer BLUE (blue moon, navy blue, royal blue). Write each answer in the grid, and the shaded column will reveal a weather feature.

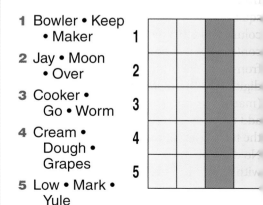

1 Bowler • Keep • Maker

2 Jay • Moon • Over

3 Cooker • Go • Worm

4 Cream • Dough • Grapes

5 Low • Mark • Yule

Mini Jigsaw

Fit the pieces in the grid to spell out a building in each row.

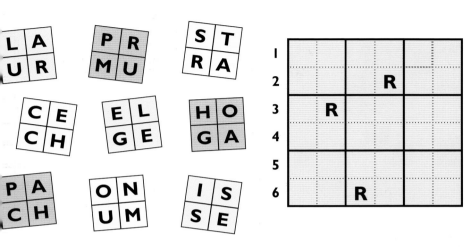

Killer Sudoku

The normal rules of Sudoku apply. Place a digit from 1-9 in each empty square so that each row, column and 3x3 block contains all the digits from 1-9. In addition, the digits in each inner shape (marked by dots) must add up to the number in the top corner of that box. No digit can be repeated within an inner shape.

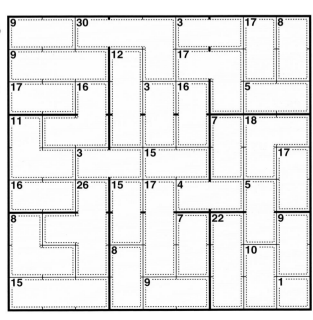

Number Jig

All but one of these numbers will fit in the grid. How quickly can you get the numbers placed?

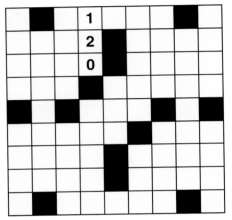

3 Digits		5 Digits
~~120~~	4380	13531
141	4523	13581
149	4621	18531
174	5522	61293
259	5555	81495
333	5596	93539
	5698	
	7698	
4 Digits	7755	**7 Digits**
1163	7913	1236789
1220	8423	1239876
1771	9142	
2183		
3516		

Mini Fit

Which one of the listed words won't fit in each of these mini grids?

ARM
BYE
MET
RUB
TIN

AND
DOG
GEL
GIN
OLD

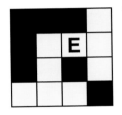

DEAR
IDOL
LAIR
LARD
ROAD

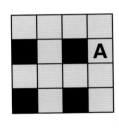

ANEW
CLAW
CODE
FEED
TALC

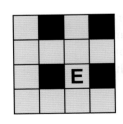

Elimination

TIME

All but two of the listed words fall into one of the four categories.
Put these leftover words together, and what word or phrase do they make?

CATEGORIES Adverbs • Young animals • Hats • SLEEP synonyms

Well	Hot	Kid	Head	Cloche	Snooze
Nap	Greedily	Slumber	Kip	Calf	Happily
Topper	Trilby	Fast	Puppy	Much	
Lamb	Doze	Chick	Bowler	Mitre	

Fare's Fair

TIME

Find two words of the same sound but different spelling to satisfy each two-element clue, then decide which of the pair goes where in the grid to discover a punctuation mark, reading down the arrowed column.

Saw the panorama

Herds of flowers

Joins the wild cat

Certain by the sea

Orchestra prohibited

Correct procedure

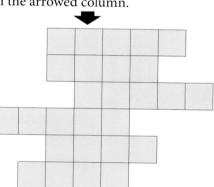

Set Square

TIME

Place one each of the digits 1-9 in the grid to make the sums work. We've put in some of the numbers to start you off. Sums should be solved from left to right, or from top to bottom.

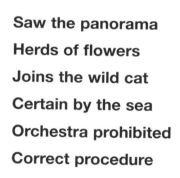

167

WORKOUT 161

Wordsearch

How quickly can you find the five themed words in each grid?

COURT

S	G	L	C	S	P	D
O	S	J	U	D	G	E
R	J	E	W	I	L	X
Z	U	U	N	A	B	J
T	R	K	I	T	V	A
H	Y	R	M	E	I	Y
F	T	K	C	O	D	W

SHOES

L	O	A	F	E	R	E
P	J	M	E	P	S	V
X	D	Y	U	B	M	O
G	F	M	G	L	I	T
R	P	F	O	O	E	K
W	N	A	R	Q	L	E
H	L	Z	B	U	C	C

Copycats

Choose the answer that best copies the pattern.

TIME

SIR is to RISK as NIL is to: Kiln • Milk • Line • Lain • Link

12 is to 3 as 16 is to: 5 • 6 • 7 • 8 • 9

OCTOPUS is to INK as SCORPION is to: Tail • Pen • Sting • Desert • Sign

DATE is to LATE as EAST is to: West • Mast • Past • Vast • Best

FLOOR is to FLOUR as BREAD is to: Dough • Bream • Knead • Breed • Wheat

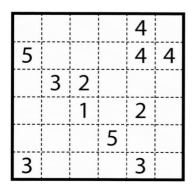

Cell Blocks

TIME

Fill the grid by drawing blocks along the gridlines. Each block must be square or rectangular and must contain the number of squares indicated by the digit inside it. Each block must contain only one digit.

Sudoku

Place a number in each empty square so that each row, each column and each 2x2 block contains all the numbers from 1-4.

	2	1	
1			2
2			3
	3	2	

4			3
		4	
3			2

2		3	4
3			2

Add Up

If the number in each circle is the sum of the two below it, how quickly can you figure out the top number? Try this one in your head, before writing anything down.

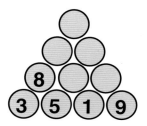

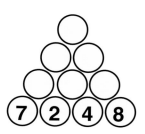

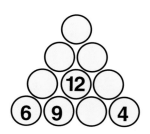

169

	10	5	12 **F**	7 **L**	26 **A**	17 **T**	17	8	15	11	5	18
26		26		26		8		2		24		15
21	8	11	16	10	15	8		8	7	26	17	8
21		1		23		17		25		18		19
26	14	8	23		19	8	26	17	3	8	15	
10		7		17		15		11				18
7	26	13	24	26	5		24	9	3	26	11	15
17				14		12		5		20		8
	21	17	26	4	7	8	15		20	10	11	5
6		26		26		8		1		26		26
11	17	25	3	13		22	7	26	21	17	8	23
19		11		8		7		5		11		8
11	5	17	8	15	12	8	15	8	5	25	8	

A̶ B C D E F̶ G H I J K L̶ M N O P Q R S T̶ U V W X Y Z

1	2	3	4	5	6	7 **L**	8	9	10	11	12 **F**	13
14	15	16	17 **T**	18	19	20	21	22	23	24	25	26 **A**

TIME

Codeword

Can you crack the code and fill in the crossword grid? Each letter of the alphabet makes at least one appearance in the grid, and is represented by the same number wherever it appears. The four letters we've decoded should help you to identify other letters and words in the grid.

Spot the Sum

TIME

In each of these boxes, one of the numbers is the sum of two others. Can you spot the sum?

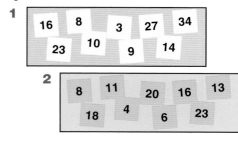

1. 16 8 3 27 34 23 10 9 14

2. 8 11 20 16 13 18 4 6 23

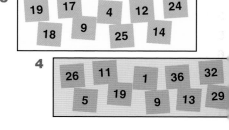

3. 19 17 4 12 24 18 9 25 14

4. 26 11 1 36 32 5 19 9 13 29

Memory Jog

Spend two minutes memorising this list of twenty words, then see how many of them you can recall on a separate piece of paper in another two minutes.

INFERIOR	CERTAIN	CLOAK	MEMORY
CARDBOARD	TRANSIENCE	SPRIG	SENSATION
SUCCESS	MERMAID	WAND	HORRIBLE
HAMMERHEAD	RHUBARB	NOMAD	POUR
NOW	KNEE	OMELETTE	LOGISTICS

Pieceword

TIME

With the help of the Across clues only, can you fit the 16 pieces into their correct positions in the empty grid (which, when completed, will exhibit a symmetrical pattern)?

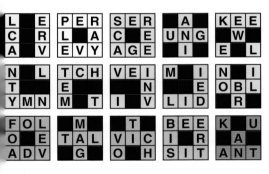

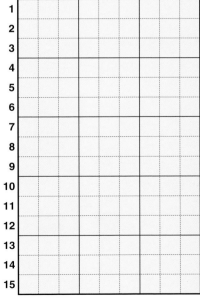

ACROSS

1 Country music • Operator

3 Bonus, benefit

5 Throw out (of a building)

6 Outdoor pool • Song of praise

8 White bathroom powder • Ladder-step

10 Blood vessel • Skin irritation

11 Distinguished

13 Honey farmer

15 Building land • Extra duty

171

Futoshiki

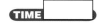

Fill the blank squares so that each row and column contains all the numbers 1, 2 and 3. Use the given numbers and the symbols that tell you if the number in the square is larger (>) or smaller (<) than the number next to it.

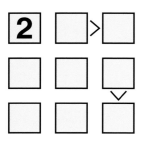

Splits

Can you rearrange each of these sets of letter blocks into a word?

1 GU MER IN ES

2 RI AN HIS TO

3 LE RIG RO MA

4 NI LE LY ENT

5 PA CH AR TRI

Disavowel

Can you complete this puzzle by adding all the vowels? There are 12 As, 7 Es, 9 Is, 11 Os and 6 Us in the puzzle.

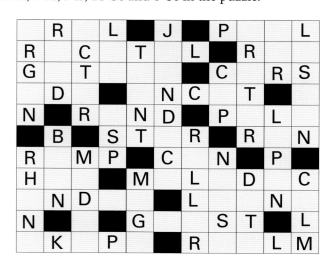

Fitword

TIME

When all of the listed words have been placed correctly in the grid, which one is left over?

3 letters
Cur
Eat
Ire
Lot
Roe
Tug
Use
Was

4 letters
Acid
Soya
Zest

5 letters
Check
Chino
Dated
Eight
Liked

Newly
~~Venom~~
Virus

7 letters
Battler
Torrent

8 letters
Gullible
Optimist

Shape Up

TIME

Can you arrange these five-letter shapes into their correct positions in the grid so that **ten composers** read down the columns?

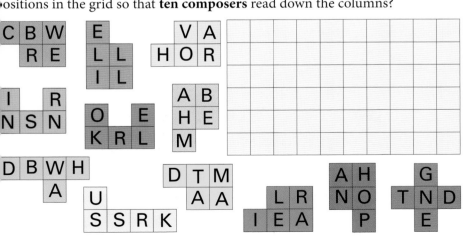

Pathfinder

TIME

Beginning with MOSEY, and moving up, down, left or right, one letter at a time, can you trace a path of 21 ways of walking?

T	Y	A	H	S	E	D	O	T	R	E
R	D	T	S	A	L	D	E	E	P	D
E	N	I	P	I	N	K	R	C	M	N
K	U	O	T	L	H	S	L	E	E	A
B	O	E	P	S	U	F	F	Y	R	A
R	E	P	M	S	E	C	N	E	B	M
A	M	L	I	T	E	F	U	S	L	E
U	B	P	O	R	K	L	O	O	M	S
L	O	M	L	H	I	W	H	C	R	T
A	T	S	L	K	L	A	E	M	A	R
T	E	S	C	U	T	T	L	E	D	I

Spot the Sum

TIME

In each of these boxes, one of the numbers is the sum of two others. Can you spot the sum?

1

29   12   16   7   10
37   23   1   21

2

8   27   34   25   5
4   10   16   23

Opposites Attract

TIME

Can you sort each set of letter blocks into two words with opposite meanings?

1 OW AD FO LE LL

2 LE LF UB HA DO

3 VE TI SS PA IVE AC

4 ACT EX TR RE ND TE

5 BE ED IO LL IE RE NT OB US

Dominoes

TIME

Solve the clues then write the six-letter answers into the dominoes. You must work out whether each word fits in clockwise or anticlockwise, so that the connecting letters of the dominoes all match up.

1 ___ Anderson, *Baywatch* star
2 ___ Garden, one of *The Goodies*
3 ___ Hawn, US actress, star of *Private Benjamin*
4 ___ Wesker, playwright
5 ___ Little, film cartoon mouse
6 ___ Clarke, *Downtown* singer

Sudoku

TIME

Use your powers of reasoning to place numbers in the grid, so that each row, each column and each 3x3 block contains the numbers 1-9.

								3
			6	2			1	7
1	4				7	8	6	
9			2	4	5			
	3	6						
2			9	3	1			
5	6				8	3	4	
			1	5		9	2	
							5	

Codewords

TIME

If DECK is 1234 and PORT is 5678, how quickly can you work out these shipping words? You should identify more letters as you go along.

1 1 6 3 4
2 3 7 2 9
3 4 2 2 10
4 11 6 10 1
5 7 12 1 1 2 7

Number Jig

Which one of the listed numbers won't fit in each of these mini grids?

192
297
298
871
917

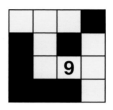

256
364
432
546
635

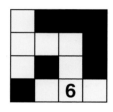

2407
4867
6402
7028
9602

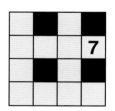

3094
5034
5127
5305
7942

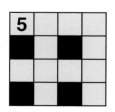

Wordsearch TIME

Hidden in this wordsearch grid are fifteen seaside words.

V	S	R	E	I	P	C	O	W
D	J	H	U	H	R	E	T	E
N	O	S	E	A	W	E	E	D
A	S	O	B	L	K	R	L	A
S	L	P	W	C	L	E	K	P
A	L	E	U	T	W	G	I	S
L	U	B	N	O	F	C	F	U
P	G	B	T	C	N	I	Z	R
M	X	L	T	I	I	Q	R	F
S	B	E	C	D	U	N	E	D
Y	D	S	E	N	Y	O	R	G

TIME

Letter Sequence

What letter should replace the question mark in these sequences?

1 A, F, C, H, E, ?

2 X, V, S, O, J, ?

3 M, O, K, Q, I, ?, G

4 O, T, T, F, F, S, ?, E, N

5 A, C, D, G, I, ?, P, U

Wild Words

What well-known phrases and expressions are suggested by these word pictures?

1 AGEBEAUTY

2

3 E
H
T
N
O

4 FULL

Smart Sums

Try to avoid writing down anything but the final answers to these calculations… no counting on fingers allowed either!

1 Minutes in an hour – syllables in PENELOPE

2 Days in 2 weeks + consonants in STANDARD

3 Vowels in VACUUM x sides on an octagon

4 Decades in a century ÷ syllables in CHRISTMAS

5 Different letters in PROCESSOR x players in a sextet

Kakuro

Simple addition and a bit of logical thinking will solve this one. You must write a digit in each white square so that the digits in each across section add up to the total in the triangle to the left, and the digits in each column add up to the total in the triangle above. 1-9 are the only digits to use and, although you may find a digit repeated in a row, it must not be repeated in the same section. We've solved one section for you.

Arroword

TIME

Just follow the arrows to write your answers in the grid. A handful of anagram clues will get you thinking differently.

Second-hand vehicle (4,3) ▼	▼	Com-mercials, in short ▼	▼	Little waves on water ▼	▼	— Cox, Radio 1 DJ	Squidgy item for the bath	Loathes	▼
Related but minor point or topic (4,5) ►					▼	▼			
DAD (anag)		DEAR (anag)		Mush ►				Plant pip	
►		▼		Burst	SPORE (anag) ►		▼		
Mushroom top ►			▼	Narrow roads ►					
Came up ►						Obtain, acquire ►			
Salesperson ►				Toboggans ►					

Small Change

TIME

Can you change one letter of each of these words to make five new words with a common theme?

1 GRILL • HAMPER • DRENCH • SEW • PLACE

2 GAVEL • BACK • BIDET • HANDED • BRAHMA

3 SHUTTER • STASH • BREAD • KNAP • TRACK

4 STARE • CERTAIN • PLAN • FAST • NODS

Futoshiki

TIME

Fill the blank squares so that each row and column contains all the numbers 1, 2 and 3. Use the given numbers and the symbols that tell you if the number in the square is larger (>) or smaller (<) than the number next to it.

Fix Six

The six birds listed will fit into this pattern of six adjoining hexagons. All are entered clockwise from a triangle to be discovered. Adjoining triangles always contain the same letter. The P gives you a start.

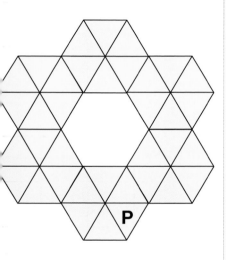

CURLEW   SHRIKE

FALCON   THRUSH

PETREL   TOUCAN

Mobile Code `TIME`

If HAIR is 4247 on this phone keypad, what other things that can be knotted have the following numbers?

1 843

2 787464

3 742266

4 268866

5 7866224

Four by Four `TIME`

How quickly can you solve these mini crosswords?

	1	2	3	4
5				
6				
7				

ACROSS

1 Bottle stopper
5 Word ending a prayer
6 Heap (of papers, e.g.,)
7 Eye swelling

DOWN

1 Peaked hats
2 Leave out
3 Depend (upon)
4 Leg joint

179

WORKOUT 173

Spot the Sum

In each of these boxes, one of the numbers is the sum of two others. Can you spot the sum?

1

9   5   29   32   18

13   21   6   25

2

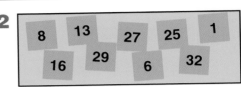

8   13   27   25   1

16   29   6   32

Splits

Can you rearrange each of these sets of letter blocks into a word?

1 BO IGH LE BS

2 SA NT GE NEW

3 AN EV CE GRI

4 NU DO TS UGH

5 LY NE RAL UT

Take Five

The three answers in this mini-crossword read the same across and down. We've clued the three answers, but not in the right order. See how quickly you can solve it.

Deadly

Creek

Civilian dress

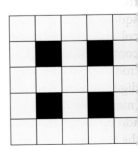

180

Mini Jigsaw

Fit the pieces in the grid to spell out a river in each row.

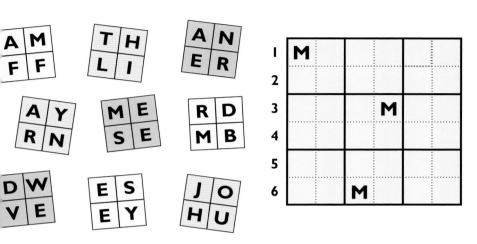

Killer Sudoku

The normal rules of sudoku apply. Place a digit from 1-9 in each empty square so that each row, column and 3x3 block contains all the digits from 1-9. In addition, the digits in each inner shape (marked by dots) must add up to the number in the top corner of that box. No digit can be repeated within an inner shape.

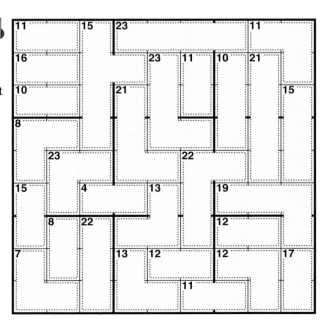

Logical

Try solving this little logical problem in your head before putting pen to paper.

Three friends met up at a Halloween fancy dress party. If Larry, not dressed as Dracula, arrived after Harry who, being a poseur, turned up as Tarzan, and Superman arrived before Dracula, when did Barry arrive and in which costume?

Staircase

When the seven **terms from the film industry** are correctly placed along the horizontal rows, the letters in the diagonal "staircase" will yield an eighth.

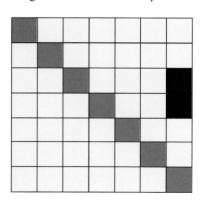

BIOPIC   FILM SET   X-RATED

BIT PART MONTAGE

COSTUME OUT-TAKE

Word Builder

Using the nine letters provided, can you answer these clues? Every answer musts include the highlighted letter B. Which standard use all nine letters?

E	H	K
A	B	C
M	N	R

5 Letters
Fossilised resin

Pair

Fracture

Park seat

Bread producer

Detox therapy

6 Letters
Supporter

Financier

Tree part

Set out on a journey

Road surface curve

Transgression (of a confidence, e.

7 Letters
Room

Tall coarse fern

Opposites Attract

Can you sort each set of letter blocks into two words with opposite meanings?

1 RK   HT   DA   LIG

2 FO   TER   AF   BE   RE

3 ED   OUD   ASH   PR   AM

4 SE   FI   RE   AR   NED   CO

Set Square

Place one each of the digits 1-9 in the grid to make the sums work. We've put in some of the numbers to start you off. Sums should be solved from left to right, or from top to bottom.

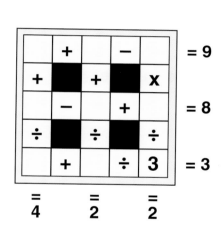

In and Out

Without changing the order of the letters, add or remove one letter each time to leave a (different) new complete word and put the added or removed letters in their respective boxes to find another name for the harmonica reading down the boxes.

TRAP		POUT	
SCOUT		GRAPE	
ROE		TIGER	
MOTOR		WHET	
BATED		BRIE	

WORKOUT 177

Wordsearch

How quickly can you find the five themed words in each grid?

HISTORY

W	S	K	X	M	O	H
I	Y	T	B	A	A	K
N	Z	W	U	N	I	R
D	H	F	O	A	U	O
S	P	V	N	R	R	Y
O	E	R	O	D	U	T
R	D	T	C	L	G	Q

GEOGRAPHY

C	T	L	C	N	D	W
R	X	O	I	H	E	F
J	U	S	T	I	S	Y
V	A	S	C	A	E	M
B	Q	N	R	G	R	K
P	K	R	A	P	T	E
T	L	E	B	D	B	Z

Three in One

The three parts of each clue lead to the same answer word. Can you solve any before you reach the third part?

1. Left • Type of wine • Harbor
2. Wolf • Scarper • Door-lock
3. Guard duty • Observe • Timepiece
4. Jalopy • Firework • Sausage
5. Lucifer • Coincide • Football game

Cell Blocks

	5				2
			3		
3			2		2
	3				
	6		4		6

Fill the grid by drawing blocks along the gridlines. Each block must be square or rectangular and must contain the number of squares indicated by the digit inside it. Each block must contain only one digit.

Sudoku [TIME]

Place a number in each empty square so that each row, each column and each 2x2 block contains all the numbers from 1-4.

	1	3	
2			1

3			4
	2	1	

			3
2			
			4
3			

Add Up [TIME]

If the number in each circle is the sum of the two below it, how quickly can you figure out the top number? Try this one in your head, before writing anything down.

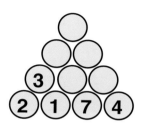

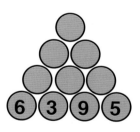

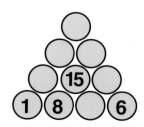

WORKOUT 179

Number Maze

Make your way from any square on the top line to any square on the bottom line. You cannot move diagonally, and every square you pass through must contain a number that divides exactly by 6.

18	10	21	66	33	96	94	54	34	36	25	12
66	97	44	90	92	18	32	42	13	26	39	68
78	34	73	42	62	24	99	36	66	78	96	66
30	24	15	18	42	30	56	68	74	86	88	18
19	36	22	36	24	66	72	96	6	27	91	24
25	54	84	18	26	72	54	84	36	67	78	6
55	24	56	52	62	68	75	74	25	92	84	26
22	60	32	18	30	42	78	24	11	82	90	11
18	30	28	24	20	88	86	48	54	42	60	33
14	40	38	96	40	22	14	34	38	10	28	80
86	96	30	42	62	22	22	22	22	22	22	22
19	18	35	23	92	22	22	22	22	22	22	22

So Complete

Complete each trio of words with a common letter. The five letters will form the answer word. Where there is a choice of completing letter, you must decide which is needed.

I_LE	LEN_	BAR_	
T_RN	POL_	_VER	
LA_E	_EAL	JA_Z	
B_AR	CH_W	HER_	
TOW_	SCA_	AC_E	

Memory Jog

Give yourself two minutes to memorise this list of thirty words. How many of them can you recall on a separate piece of paper in another two minutes?

PHOBIA	CUSHION	SPORT	LOCKET
FRIENDLY	WILLOW	RIPPLE	DUMB-BELL
ATTITUDE	SANDAL	CHARIOT	FIN
CLEARLY	COUGHING	BUCKLE	DARING
EXPECT	FORTUNATE	TALL	MAYONNAISE
DECISION	SCRATCH	BEADS	CRUMBLE
MOOR	QUEASY	SHRILL	
SWORD	DANGLE	DIGITAL	

Number Jig

All but one of these numbers will fit in the grid. How quickly can you get the numbers placed?

3 Digits
287
359
887
533
533
839

4 Digits
312
452
2518
2649
3434

4 Digits
3441
3443
3649
4512
4538
4542
5438
5563
6434
6448
9827
9842

5 Digits
25428
25437
28231
28321
33157
33257

7 Digits
3456543
5432345

Scramble TIME

What birds can be made from each of these sets of scrambled letters?

1 LOW
2 SO EGO
3 PINE GUN
4 OF CLAN
5 RANG LIST
6 HEAT SNAP
7 SALT BOARS
8 WE ROPE DOCK

Initials TIME

If ITHOTN (Oscar-winning film) is *IN THE HEAT OF THE NIGHT*, what do these initials represent?

1 SOL (American landmark)
2 LOTV (Flower)
3 TMOV (Shakespeare play)
4 PIB (Rolling Stones song)
5 KCS (Breed of dog)

Honeycomb TIME

Write the six-letter answers clockwise round their respective cell-numbers, starting at the arrowed cell. On completion, you will find that the unclued answers (10 and 11) will reveal a three-word phrase meaning "at no cost."

1 Previously
2 Elevenses drink
3 Spidery, untidy handwriting
4 Bull's noise
5 Look for diligently
6 Photographer's instrument
7 Thin
8 Sleep intermittently – like puss?
9 Repudiate

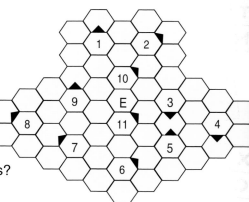

Fitword

TIME

When all of the listed words have been placed correctly in the grid, which one is left over?

letters	5 letters	8 letters
lu	Evict	Butchery
np	~~Mufti~~	Cheering
nk	Nymph	Narrator
ia	Taken	Splicing
letters	7 letters	Thuggery
Gang	Needier	**11 letters**
Smut	Plateau	Interacting

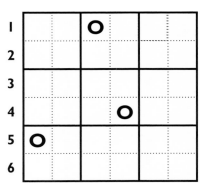

Mini Jigsaw

TIME

Fit the pieces in the grid to spell out the name of a writer in each row.

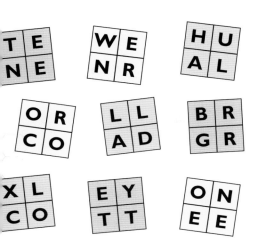

189

Wordsearch

If you're planning a skiing trip this year you may become familiar with some of the words and phrases associated with ski resorts, found in the grid. There are thirteen words for you to find.

N	I	A	T	N	U	O	M	H
A	C	C	U	A	S	D	G	C
G	H	B	A	L	E	I	H	D
G	U	L	O	B	E	A	C	R
O	T	P	C	L	I	S	U	A
B	E	E	S	R	E	N	R	C
O	S	B	L	T	F	I	L	B
T	O	I	A	A	X	W	I	W
B	F	K	J	Q	H	O	N	C
T	S	L	U	G	E	C	G	N
A	P	R	E	S	S	K	I	S

Number Jig

Which one of the listed numbers won't fit in each of these mini grids?

137
267
417
724
737

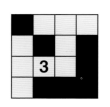

157
351
357
371
713

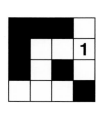

2935
3949
5229
5392
9235

Pairs

Pair off 24 of the listed words to form twelve "double-barrelled" words and rearrange the letters of the two words left over to reveal a medicinal preparation.

APPLE	CUSTARD	HARD	PIANO	SWITCH
BEST	EGG	LIGHT	PLATES	TITLE
BOILED	FIGHT	MASTER	POWER	
BOY	FRIEND	MOSS	SCHOOL	
CHEESE	GLASSES	NIGHT	STATION	
COURTESY	GRAND	OPERA	SUNDAY	

Manor Born

TIME

Which numbered photo has been taken?

Sudoku

TIME

Use your powers of reasoning to place numbers in the grid, so that each row, each column and each 3x3 block contains the numbers 1-9.

	6						9	8
	5	4	7		1			
1						7	2	
8			5	1	3			
	3							
4			7	9	6			
9						2	7	
	2	6	8		4			
	4						5	9

Splits

TIME

Can you rearrange each of these sets of letter blocks into a word?

1 MAT AU IC TO

2 RY SE TA CRE

3 TU AL NOC RN

4 VE BLE TA GE

5 LY AR QU TER

Word Builder TIME

Using the nine letters provided, can you answer these clues? Every answer must include the highlighted letter L. Which piece of exercise equipment uses all nine letters?

L	I	D
E	**L**	M
T	A	R

5 Letters
Volume measurement
Wide awake
Roofer
River mouth
Afterwards
Perfect

6 Letters
Sell
Posted
Wooden hammer
Ring again
Small particular
Corn grinder

7 Letters
Word for word, to the letter
Followed
Agreed

8 Letters
Tested

Wordsearch TIME

Hidden in this wordsearch grid are fifteen chocolate words.

Z	B	M	Q	K	Y	Z	W	E
C	H	O	I	C	E	R	F	T
M	U	E	N	L	A	A	U	I
A	I	U	N	P	K	E	D	H
E	T	F	P	I	D	R	G	W
R	C	E	G	W	L	E	E	T
C	R	O	J	O	E	A	F	L
D	S	H	F	F	V	O	R	M
A	T	A	F	F	S	X	C	P
R	X	O	B	R	E	Y	A	L
K	T	M	E	N	U	E	P	N

Codewords TIME

If BEACH is 12345 and SHORE is 65782, how quickly can you work out these beach words? You should identify more letters as you go along.

1 6 2 3

2 4 8 3 1

3 4 7 3 6 9

4 8 2 6 7 8 9

5 1 3 9 5 2 8 6

Memory Jog

Give yourself two minutes to memorise this list of words –
twenty-five this time! How many of them can you recall on
a separate piece of paper in another two minutes?

MIGHT	TABLE	BELL	ORCHESTRA	SHEEP
CUPBOARD	RAIN	SHIPYARD	POLITE	WALL
CING	FORWARD	EVENLY	BEHIND	MAJORITY
PLAICE	REVENGE	MASK	GREEN	PADDLE
SINCERTITY	TONE	WANDER	DUSTY	REMINDER

Small Change

Can you change one letter of each of these words to make five
new words with a common theme?

1 DIRE • DANGER • SPEAK • MALE • CLUE

2 BIN • BARGE • BRAND • VASE • HUGS

3 MANGE • TEXT • BASIS • BUTTON • TAP

4 SPINE • NAME • ATTAR • CREPT • SEW

Kakuro

Simple addition and a bit of logical thinking will solve this one. You must write
a digit in each white square so that the digits in each across section add up to
the total in the triangle to the left, and the digits in each column add up to the
total in the triangle above. 1-9 are the only digits to use and, although you may
find a digit repeated in a row, it must not be repeated in the same section.
We've solved one section for you.

WORKOUT 187

Arroword

Just follow the arrows to write your answers in the grid. A handful of anagram clues will get you thinking differently.

TAILED (anag) ▼	Letters after a firm's name (abbr) ▼	▼	— Norman, golfer	▼	Part of cauliflower or broccoli	▼	Give extra vigor or spirit to	Very much (4,2)
Conflict (with) ►					▼			▼
Sharp poke	BARS (anag)		2003 Will Ferrell film ►				Theatre in Dublin	
►		▼	Large antelope	Narrow valley	►		▼	
Family —, genealogy chart ►		▼		Bring up (young)	►			
►			Undershirts ►					
Cure	Mr Blue —, ELO hit ►			— Walcott, Arsenal player ►				

Scramble

The names of which type of dining venue can be made from each of these sets of scrambled letters? I think this calls for a cream cake!

1 RAB

2 NIN

3 FACE

4 ROBS IT

5 EAR YET

6 NEAR VAT

7 SHYER LOT

8 BRAISE RES

Initials

If ITHOTN (Oscar-winning film) is *IN THE HEAT OF THE NIGHT*, what do these initials represent?

1 OFITG (Sitcom)

2 WAM (Composer)

3 HAS (Children's game)

4 YOLT (Bond film)

5 ASITSN (Proverb)

Mini Fit

Which one of the listed words won't fit in each of these mini grids?

ANT
ART
NAG
ROT
TOR

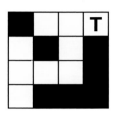

DEN
END
PEN
PET
PIE

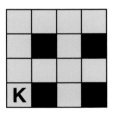

DAWN
LAWN
WALK
WEAK
WIDE

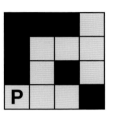

ELSE
SEEN
SLOW
SWAT
TWIN

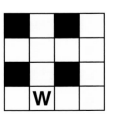

Vowel Play

Can you replace the missing vowels to complete the names of these musical instruments?

1 V L N
2 T R M P T
3 G T R
4 C C R D N
5 P N

6 B
7 B S S N
8 F L T
9 R G N
10 C L L

Set Square

Place one each of the digits 1-9 in the grid to make the sums work. We've put in some of the numbers to start you off. Sums should be solved from left to right, or from top to bottom.

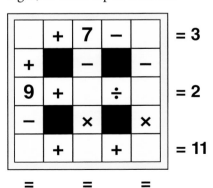

WORKOUT 189

Spot the Sum

In each of these boxes, one of the numbers is the sum of two others. Can you spot the sum?

1

21   4   30   16   10
24   7   27   8

3

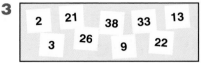

2   21   38   33   13
3   26   9   22

2

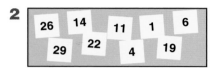

26   14   11   1   6
29   22   4   19

4

22   7   44   33   35
18   21   12   27

Box Wise

Can you place the three-letter groups in the boxes, so that neighbouring boxes always make a six-letter word, like PAR-DON or DON-ATE? We've placed one group to start you off.

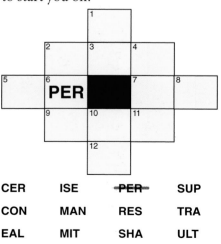

CER	ISE	~~PER~~	SUP
CON	MAN	RES	TRA
EAL	MIT	SHA	ULT

Staircase

When the seven TV programmes are correctly placed along the horizontal rows, the letters in the diagonal "staircase" will yield an eighth.

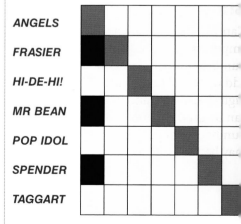

ANGELS

FRASIER

HI-DE-HI!

MR BEAN

POP IDOL

SPENDER

TAGGART

196

Mini Jigsaw

Fit the pieces in the grid to spell out a part of a car in each row.

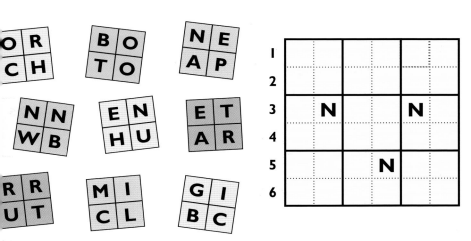

Six Pack

Can you place digits in the empty triangles, so that the numbers in each hexagon add up to 25? Only single digits between 1 and 9 can be used, and no two numbers in any hexagon may be the same.

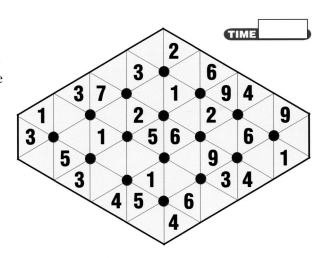

SOLUTIONS

WORKOUT 1
WORDSEARCH

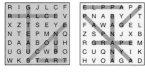

SPLITS
1 Discovery 2 Tolerated
3 Solicitor 4 Longitude
5 Whichever

CELL BLOCKS

WORKOUT 2
SUDOKU

3	4	2	1
2	1	4	3
4	3	1	2
1	2	3	4

2	4	1	3
1	3	2	4
4	1	3	2
3	2	4	1

3	4	2	1
1	2	4	3
4	1	3	2
2	3	1	4

ADD UP
1 48 2 35 3 26

WORKOUT 3
CODEWORD

SPOT THE SUM
1 33 (14+19) 2 33 (12+21)
3 21 (3+18) 4 34 (6+28)

WORKOUT 4
PYRAMID
1 I 2 It 3 Tie 4 Tier
5 Inert 6 Retina 7 Terrain
8 Restrain 9 Arresting

WORKOUT 5
FUTOSHIKI

1	3	2	4
3	4	1	2
2	1	4	3
4	2	3	1

INITIALS
1 *When I'm Cleaning Windows* 2 *Three Blind Mice* 3 *The Lord of the Rings* 4 *The Lion, The Witch and the Wardrobe* 5 *Hard candy*

SHIKAKU

WORKOUT 6
FITWORD

Leftover word: **HIT**

SIX PACK

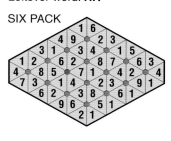

WORKOUT 7
PATHFINDER

NUMBER JIG
1 324 2 469 3 3131

COPYCATS
1 Speak 2 Drey 3 Caddy
4 Mule (change the 2nd letter to the 6th after it in the alphabet)

WORKOUT 8
DOMINOES
1 Marina 2 Bernie 3 Albert
4 Teresa 5 Creole 6 Arnold

SUDOKU

8	3	6	9	2	1	4	5	7
5	9	4	3	6	7	8	2	1
2	7	1	4	5	8	6	9	3
3	8	9	5	1	6	2	7	4
1	2	7	8	3	4	5	6	9
6	4	5	2	7	9	3	1	8
4	6	3	7	9	2	1	8	5
9	1	8	6	4	5	7	3	2
7	5	2	1	8	3	9	4	6

CODEWORDS
1 Charm (of finches)
2 Crash (of rhinoceroses)
3 Swarm (of bees)
4 Murder (of crows)
5 Pride (of lions) (8=C, 9=S, 10=W, 11=U, 12=P, 13=I)

WORKOUT 9

MINI FIT
1 Tic **2** Rod **3** Five **4** Erne

WORDSEARCH

A	P	T	L	B	A	N	J	O
R	S	E	G	N	O	G	P	N
I	I	N	A	P	M	I	T	A
S	T	I	T	P	C	U	T	I
M	L	R	R	C	B	E	V	P
D	F	A	O	A	P	J	I	E
R	H	L	B	M	L	H	O	O
U	O	C	U	M	B	O	L	B
M	F	R	Y	T	Y	O	I	O
S	T	O	L	L	E	C	N	V
G	U	I	T	A	R	B	G	E

Banjo, Cello, Clarinet, Cymbals, Drums, Flute, Gong, Guitar, Harp, Oboe, Piano, Piccolo, Timpani, Trombone, Trumpet, Tuba, Viola, Violin

SCRAMBLE
1 Rome **2** Paris **3** Athens **4** Copenhagen **5** Bucharest **6** Budapest **7** Amsterdam **8** Bratislava

WORKOUT 10

SMALL CHANGE
1 Ford, Rover, Fiat, Seat, Lexus **2** Rose, Daisy, Lily, Iris, Pansy **3** Gold, Silver, Tin, Iron, Lead **4** Table, Chair, Desk, Chest, Dresser

OPPOSITES ATTRACT
1 Empty/Full
2 Finish/Start
3 Difficult/Simple
4 Precise/Vague

KAKURO

	3	1		8	9		8	1
3	1	2	5	4	7	8	9	6
1	2		1	3		9	7	

WORKOUT 11

ARROWORD

S	F	G		W		
P	R	O	M	I	S	E	F
E		G		L	E	A	V	E
W	E	B		B	A	K	E	R
	C	R	I	M	E		E	R	R
C	H	I	C		R	A	N	G	E
	M	E	L	T		S	E	T

VOWEL PLAY
1 Carrot **2** Potato
3 Lettuce **4** Pea **5** Leek **6** Kale
7 Onion **8** Celery **9** Radish
10 Beetroot

SMART SUMS
1 30 (5 x 6) **2** 16 (64÷4)
3 37 (50-13) **4** 11 (4+7)

WORKOUT 12

EGG-TIMER
1 Hearts **2** Share **3** Rash
4 Ash **5** As **6** Sea **7** Peas
8 Spade **9** Spades

MOBILE CODE
1 Cap **2** Beret **3** Panama
4 Trilby **5** Bowler

FOUR BY FOUR

B	O	L	T
A	R	I	A
T	A	L	K
S	L	O	E

WORKOUT 13

SET SQUARE

3	+	7	−	2
−		+		×
1	+	9	−	6
×		÷		+
5	×	4	−	8

IN AND OUT
Cares (- S), cache (+ C), herd (- A), rifle (+ L), scream (+ E) **SCALE**
Rap (- M), coroner (+ O), brand (+ D), case (- E), bind (- L)**MODEL**

BOX WISE
1 Cor **2** Out **3** Set **4** Tee
5 Rep **6** Lay **7** The **8** Ory
9 Man **10** Tra **11** Nce **12** Vel

WORKOUT 14

MINI JIGSAW
Gannet, Osprey, Grouse, Oriole, Cuckoo, Plover

KILLER SUDOKU

7	2	5	8	3	1	6	9	4
1	6	3	4	9	2	8	5	7
4	8	9	6	5	7	2	1	3
6	1	2	7	4	5	3	8	9
8	3	4	2	1	9	7	6	5
9	5	7	3	8	6	1	4	2
2	7	8	5	6	4	9	3	1
5	9	6	1	2	3	4	7	8
3	4	1	9	7	8	5	2	6

WORKOUT 15

STAIRCASE
Hayrick, Arable, Farmer, Drovers, Yield, Crops, Piglet.

The word is: **HARVEST**

NUMBER SEQUENCE
1 49 (sum of previous two numbers, take away 1) **2** 5 (letters in name of numbers one, two, three etc) **3** 2732 (x4, -4) **4** 5040 (x1, x2, x3 etc) **5** 1093 (x3,+1)

WORD BUILDER
Tiger, Irate, Might, Eater, Eight, Gather, Either, Metier, Heater, Gaiter, Ragtime, Meatier, Emirate, Emigrate, Heritage, Hermitage

SOLUTIONS

WORKOUT 16
WILD WORDS
1 Think twice **2** Rock around the clock **3** Hole in one **4** Broad bean

FARE'S FAIR

R	O	S	E	
C	H	E	C	K
M	A	R	E	
W	R	I	T	E
	S	A	W	
T	O	L	D	

ELIMINATION
Dairy – Brie, Cheese, Milk, Whey, Yogurt.
HAND – Cuff, Made, Set, Shake, Some.
Gases – Argon, Hydrogen, Methane, Neon, Oxygen.
Boxing – Corner, Gloves, Ring, Ropes, Spar.

Leftover phrase: **WELL DONE**

WORKOUT 17
NINERS
Telescope, worldwide, inelegant, gondolier
The left-hand column gives **TWIG**.

CELL BLOCKS

	4			4
3		1		
	4	4		
	4	2		6
	4			

WORKOUT 18
SUDOKU

4	2	3	1
3	1	4	2
1	4	2	3
2	3	1	4

2	3	1	4
1	4	2	3
3	1	4	2
4	2	3	1

4	2	3	1
3	1	4	2
2	3	1	4
1	4	2	3

ADD UP
1 38 **2** 42 **3** 48

WORKOUT 19
CODEWORD

COPY CATS
1 Open **2** Sun **3** PQRS (1st letter to 4th) **4** Drive **5** Taps (reorder letters into new positions)

WORKOUT 20
SPLITS
1 Beefsteak **2** Unlimited **3** Redundant **4** Signature **5** Godmother

SHAPE UP

R	T	G	S	B	R	I	T	R	S
O	U	I	T	R	E	N	I	U	I
T	R	O	U	A	N	G	T	B	S
H	N	T	B	Q	O	R	I	E	L
K	E	T	B	U	I	E	A	N	E
O	R	O	S	E	R	S	N	S	Y

WORKOUT 21
FUTOSHIKI

1	3	2	4
3	4	1	2
2	1	4	3
4	2	3	1

SCRAMBLE
1 Shoe **2** Spat **3** Skate **4** Gaiter **5** Brogue **6** Slipper **7** Espadrille **8** Wellington

PET TALK
Photograph 2

WORKOUT 22
FITWORD

S		A			C		S
H	O	L	T		D	R	A	T
A		M		I	E		O
D	I	S	E	M	B	A	R	K
E				M	M		E
	A	C	R	O	N	Y	M
S		O		R			A
C	A	S	C	A	D	I	N	G
O		T		L	M	I	
U	G	L	Y		M	A	L	L
T		Y			M		E

Kitty

MIND THE GAP
Tetanus, Academy, Acrobat, Adamant, Forever, Instead, Affirms, Awaking.

The creature is:
AARDVARK

WORKOUT 23
PATHFINDER

PIRATE SHIP, TRIMARAN, SKIFF, CORACLE, PRIVATEER, CLIPPER, SLOOP, NARROWBOAT, HOUSEBOAT, FERRY, CAIQUE, BATTLESHIP, BARGE, GALLEON, DHOW, MOTORBOAT, CANOE

SOUNDALIKES
1 Threw/through **2** Poor/paw **3** Where/wear

HONEYCOMB
1 Degree **2** Drudge **3** Beware! **4** Darwin **5** Coward **6** People **7** Pulpit **8** Hamper **9** Lumber **10&11** George Orwell

WORKOUT 24
SET SQUARE

9	×	2	−	1
+		×		+
7	+	8	÷	5
−		÷		+
3	×	4	−	6

SUDOKU

8	2	3	9	1	4	5	6	7
6	9	4	7	8	5	3	1	2
5	7	1	6	2	3	8	9	4
3	5	9	4	7	2	6	8	1
4	8	7	1	3	6	2	5	9
2	1	6	5	9	8	4	7	3
7	4	2	8	5	9	1	3	6
1	3	5	2	6	7	9	4	8
9	6	8	3	4	1	7	2	5

INITIALS
1 A friend in need is a friend indeed 2 The Old Curiosity Shop 3 He's from Barcelona 4 One Flew Over the Cuckoo's Nest 5 Bread and butter pudding

WORKOUT 25
SIX SIX

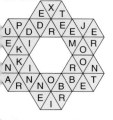

WORDSEARCH

PICTURE PAIR
1 and 5

WORKOUT 26
NUMBER JIG
1 439 2 165 3 7239

SMALL CHANGE
1 Scone, Tart, Bun, Cake, Pie 2 Tarn, Lake, Pool, Pond, Mere 3 Stone, Pound, Ton, Gram, Ounce 4 Shorts, Skirt, Kilt, Gown, Dress

KAKURO

WORKOUT 27
ARROWORD

A		S		O		M	
S	A	T	S	U	M	A	R
S		Y		T	E	R	S	E
J	U	T			C	L	A	M	P
R	A	D	A	R		C	I	A
R	E	L	Y		O	V	A	L	S
		K	E	L	P		S	E	T

TAKE FIVE

T	I	B	I	A
I		A		L
B	A	N	A	L
I		A		O
A	L	L	O	W

TWO OF A KIND
1 Decent/Proper 2 Choice/Special 3 Caretaker/Janitor 4 Pinpoint/Spot 5 Impromptu/Spontaneous

WORKOUT 28
WORDSEARCH

Y	L	E	V	P	U	H
Z	S	L	E	E	T	A
D	W	Z	S	A	Q	I
O	M	Z	B	N	S	L
R	C	I	I	F	O	H
K	J	R	N	T	G	W
X	E	D	T	S	I	M

K	A	S	P	X	Z	Y
F	P	H	C	A	S	U
L	H	A	F	O	O	L
I	W	M	D	H	M	S
B	O	P	Q	C	L	V
S	P	O	N	G	E	R
J	E	O	T	N	G	G

N	P	B	U	F	F	V
A	V	O	N	G	A	E
E	B	T	L	R	P	M
L	D	J	N	I	Q	S
C	F	I	W	Z	S	R
X	S	A	H	E	I	H
H	L	C	O	Y	W	P

VOWEL PLAY
1 Doctors 2 Spooks 3 Coast 4 Hustle 5 Newsnight 6 Casualty 7 Morse 8 Lost 9 Panorama 10 Countdown

THREE IN ONE
1 Score 2 Bear 3 Lay 4 Drive 5 Slide

WORKOUT 29
MISSING LINK
1 Wide 2 Star 3 Care 4 Bath 5 Test. The game is: DARTS

CODEWORDS
1 Eagle 2 Hole 3 Ball 4 Birdie 5 Wood 6 Wedge (9=E, 10=H, 11=B, 12=D, 13=W)

MIND THE GAP
1 Pet 2 Ore 3 Add 4 Fun 5 Dig

WORKOUT 30
MINI JIGSAW
Purple, Silver, Yellow Orange, Violet, Indigo

KILLER SUDOKU

3	6	4	5	2	7	8	1	9
1	9	7	3	8	6	2	5	4
8	5	2	1	9	4	7	6	3
2	7	6	4	3	8	1	9	5
9	8	3	6	1	5	4	2	7
5	4	1	9	7	2	6	3	8
7	3	5	2	4	1	9	8	6
6	2	8	7	5	9	3	4	1
4	1	9	8	6	3	5	7	2

SOLUTIONS

WORKOUT 31
MINI FIT
1 Tip **2** Mat **3** Tube **4** Deaf

WORD BUILDER
Teach, Scare, Chore, Chest, Chaos, Chase, Search, Actors, Caster, Corset, Coarser, Torches, Coaster, Archers, Creators, Reactors, Orchestra

WORKOUT 32
SPLITS
1 Porcupine **2** Dishonest
3 Bookplate **4** Companion
5 Smugglers. The bonus link is kitchen words within the words – Cup, Dish, Plate, Pan, Mug

PAIRS
Bank holiday, bottle-opener, campfire, cheese biscuit, cupboard, insurance claim, lemon tea, necklace, ponytail, skin-diving, squash racket, stopcock
LEANT and MOWER yield WATER MELON

WORKOUT 33
WORDSEARCH

SET SQUARE

6	−	2	+	5
×		×		+
4	×	9	÷	3
−		−		−
8	+	7	−	1

CELL BLOCKS

	2		4
		3	
	2		6
		1	
6	6		6

WORKOUT 34
SUDOKU

1	3	2	4
2	4	1	3
4	1	3	2
3	2	4	1

4	1	3	2
3	2	4	1
2	4	1	3
1	3	2	4

3	1	2	4
2	4	3	1
1	2	4	3
4	3	1	2

ADD UP
1 36
2 42
3 60

WORKOUT 35
CODEWORD

SO COMPLETE

Safe	golf,	lift	F
Pain,	pier,	chip	I
Wage,	gear,	ring	G
Ache,	chef,	heal	H
Stem,	halt,	fist	T

WORKOUT 36
SPLITS
1 Playhouse **2** Confident
3 Perishing **4** Remainder
5 Omelettes

PIECEWORD

WORKOUT 37
LETTER SEQUENCE
1 N (+3, +4, +5 etc) **2** C (-2, +1, -3, +1, -4, +1 etc) **3** M (+3, -3, -3, +3, +7, -7, -7, +7) **4** I (+10, -8, +10, - etc) **5** E (-1, -2, -3 etc)

MOBILE CODE
1 Bath **2** Hull **3** York
4 Leeds **5** Dundee
6 Cardiff

DISAVOWEL

WORKOUT 38
FITWORD

Play

SMART SUMS
1 180 (3x60) **2** 18 (13+5)
3 36 (4x9) **4** 60 (360÷6)
5 8 (13-5)

WORKOUT 39
PATHFINDER

MARTIN, BERNARD,
ALEXANDER, PAUL, LOUIS,
BENEDICT, ANNE, THOMAS,
ELIZABETH, LUCY, JOSEPH,
HELEN, BARTHOLOMEW,
THERESA, DANIEL, DAVID,
PETER, FRANCIS, GABRIEL

BOX WISE

1 Mut **2** Car **3** Ton **4** Sil
5 Lea **6** Ves **7** Ver **8** Bal
9 Tal **10** Ent **11** Ity **12** Ail

LOGICAL

1st Aidan, Red Rose,
2nd Connor, Desert Dahlia,
3rd Brendan, Lilac Lilac

WORKOUT 40
SET SQUARE

4	×	6	−	8
×	■	+	■	−
9	+	1	÷	5
÷	■	×	■	+
3	×	2	+	7

SUDOKU

1	6	4	3	7	9	2	8	5
9	2	7	6	8	5	4	3	1
3	8	5	2	4	1	9	6	7
8	7	2	9	5	6	1	4	3
4	5	1	8	2	3	6	7	9
6	3	9	7	1	4	5	2	8
5	1	6	4	3	8	7	9	2
7	9	8	5	6	2	3	1	4
2	4	3	1	9	7	8	5	6

STAIRCASE

Menzies, Barclay, Scott,
Ogilvy, Maxwell, Cameron,
Lamond. The "staircase"
reveals: **MACLEOD**

WORKOUT 41
MINI FIT

1 Net **2** Pip **3** Tape **4** Blur

WORD SEARCH

SCRAMBLE

1 Boxer **2** Beagle **3** Poodle
4 Pointer **5** Whippet
6 Lurcher **7** Alsatian
8 Pekinese

WORKOUT 42
NINERS

Discourse, architect,
withstand, Norwegian
The left-hand column gives
DAWN.

KAKURO

		9	3	8	1		2	1
9	8	5	1	7	2	4	6	3
7	9		6	9	4	8		

WORKOUT 43
ARROWORD

INITIALS

1 Keep off the grass **2** Jack
and the Beanstalk **3** Many
hands make light work
4 The Phantom of the
Opera **5** Butch Cassidy
and the Sundance Kid

NUMBER SEQUENCE

1 26 (+1, +3, +5...) **2** 60
(-10, -9, -8...) **3** 34 (x2, -1,
x2, -1...) **4** 122 (x3-1) **5** 100
(Value of British coins)

WORKOUT 44
DOMINOES

1 Rupert **2** Arthur
3 Thomas **4** Maxine
5 Joanne **6** Joseph

MOBILE CODE

1 Blue **2** Gold **3** Pink
4 Green **5** Purple

FOUR BY FOUR

WORKOUT 45
FARE'S FAIR

	B	U	Y	E	R
S	I	G	N	E	T
	S	E	N	T	
T	H	Y	M	E	
M	O	U	R	N	
	P	L	A	C	E

FUTOSHIKI

2	1	3
3	2	1
1	3	2

STAIRCASE

Ravioli, Honey, Sausage,
Hobnob, Cereal, Butter,
Kebab. Edible item:
RHUBARB

SOLUTIONS

WORKOUT 46
MINI JIGSAW
Fennel, Celery, Turnip
Carrot, Potato, Marrow

KILLER SUDOKU

9	5	2	7	4	8	3	6	1
4	3	1	2	9	6	5	7	8
8	6	7	1	3	5	4	2	9
6	9	5	3	8	4	2	1	7
1	8	3	9	7	2	6	5	4
7	2	4	5	6	1	9	8	3
2	7	8	4	5	9	1	3	6
3	1	9	6	2	7	8	4	5
5	4	6	8	1	3	7	9	2

WORKOUT 47
SUDOKU

3	1	2	4		2	1	3	4
4	2	1	3		4	3	2	1
2	3	4	1		1	2	4	3
1	4	3	2		3	4	1	2

3	1	4	2
2	4	1	3
4	2	3	1
1	3	2	4

WORD BUILDER
Canoe, Camel, Panic, Mince,
Clean, Pecan, Pencil, Plaice,
Cinema, Income, In place,
Pelican, Complain, Policeman

WORKOUT 48
ALPHA-FIT

SIX PACK

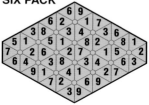

SPOT THE SUM
1 22 (15+7) **2** 29 (18+11)
3 30 (18+12) **4** 35 (29+6)

WORKOUT 49
ELIMINATION

Musical instruments –
Bassoon, Cornet, Cymbals,
Triangle, Viola.
PIECE – Conversation, Hair,
Master, Party, Time.
No vowels – Crypt, Lynx,
Myrrh, Rhythm, Why.
Reptiles – Alligator, Anaconda,
Cobra, Iguana, Turtle.
Leftover phrase: **SQUARE
MEAL**

LOGICAL

Colin, Ironing, Wednesday
Andrew, Dusting, Tuesday
Brian, Gardening, Monday

CELL BLOCKS

WORKOUT 50
WORDSEARCH

ADD UP
1 31 **2** 25 **3** 41

WORKOUT 51
CODEWORD

J	O	Y	L	E	S	S		S	C	A	B
T	D		A		H		I		O		E
W	E	E	P	Y		O	R	G	A	N	Z	A
I			E		D		U		F		K
S	Q	U	A	R	E	D		A	G	O	G
T		X			Y		N		R		W
E	X	T	E	N	D		W	A	R	M	T	H
D		R		E		B		O			E
	N	O	V	A		O	U	T	D	O	N	E
O		T		R		L		R			D
B	O	T	T	L	E	D		A	T	O	L	L
E		E		Y		L		I		A		E
Y	A	R	D		M	Y	S	T	E	R	Y

SOUNDALIKES
1 Caught/Court
2 Heard/Herd
3 Which/Witch
4 Knows/Nose

WORKOUT 52
SPLITS
1 Alligator **2** Xylophone
3 Sandpaper **4** Marmalade
5 Potential

SHAPE UP

B	E	H	K	F	M	G	W	K	M
A	K	A	I	A	I	R	E	I	O
C	L	R	D	R	R	A	A	N	N
A	A	L	M	R	R	B	V	S	R
L	N	O	A	O	E	L	E	K	O
L	D	W	N	W	N	E	R	I	E

WORKOUT 53
TWO OF A KIND
1 Sailor/Seaman **2** Forbid/
Prohibit **3** Conjurer/
Magician **4** Oversee/
Supervise **5** Defender/
Guardian

CODEWORDS
1 Peat **2** Potato **3** Shoots
(7=S) **4** Petal (8=L) **5** Apple

STAR TURN
Photograph 1

WORKOUT 54

FITWORD

S	I	G	H	T	S	E	E
E	R		E		E		M
C	I	K	K	A		E	Y	E
C		D		I	M		R
U	F	F	Y		I	C	Y
	U		N			
V	A	R		R	I	G	I	D
	L	I	E				O
P	R	O		N	A	V	A	L
	N		A		E		E
R	E	G	U	L	A	T	E

Tactile

SET SQUARE

6	÷	2	+	8
+				−
9	−	4	+	1
−		×		÷
5	−	3	×	7

WORKOUT 55

PATHFINDER

C	H	I	S	R	O	S	E	M	A	R
S	E	V	E	E	N	N	E	I	S	Y
A	V	R	R	L	E	G	F	L	A	C
E	G	A	A	T	G	A	I	C	B	H
L	O	C	H	I	A	R	L	L	I	E
Y	N	O	R	C	S	M	O	C	V	R
A	A	G	E	O	R	A	R	R	E	D
B	N	O	Y	R	O	J	I	V	E	N
E	M	M	C	M	A	R	A	A	E	L
H	Y	I	O	R	E	D	N	L	Y	S
T	T	N	M	F	R	E	Y	P	A	R

CHICORY, COMFREY,
PARSLEY, LAVENDER,
CORIANDER, MARJORAM,
SAGE, GARLIC, BASIL,
FENNEL, TARRAGON,
OREGANO, MINT, THYME,
BAY LEAVES, CHIVES,
ROSEMARY, CHERVIL

PYRAMID

1 R 2 Ra 3 Era
4 Care 5 Cater 6 Trance
7 Certain 8 Canister
9 Miscreant

WORKOUT 56

MIND THE GAP

Vacancy, Gorilla, Cabbage,
Acrobat, Eclipse, Twinkle,
Earlier, Stencil. Musical
instrument: **CLARINET**

SUDOKU

1	9	6	8	2	7	5	4	3
2	4	8	5	6	3	9	1	7
5	7	3	4	1	9	2	8	6
6	3	9	7	8	4	1	2	5
4	5	1	2	9	6	7	3	8
7	8	2	1	3	5	6	9	4
9	1	5	3	7	8	4	6	2
8	6	7	9	4	2	3	5	1
3	2	4	6	5	1	8	7	9

THREE IN ONE

1 Fair 2 Drive 3 Neck 4 Blue
5 Part

WORKOUT 57

MINI FIT

1 Paw 2 Cod 3 Done 4 Drop

WORD SEARCH

VOWEL PLAY

1 Moth 2 Mosquito 3 Midge
4 Beetle 5 Locust 6 Termite
7 Gnat 8 Cicada 9 Earwig
10 Aphid

WORKOUT 58

SMART SUMS

1 36 (4x9) 2 33 (26+7)
3 30 (90÷3) 4 11 (5+6) 5 6 (8-2)

MIND THE GAP

1 Ace 2 Lot 3 Pin 4 One
5 The

KAKURO

3	1		4	1	6	2	
1	2	5	9	3	8	6	4	7
	1	7	2	9		8	9

WORKOUT 59

ARROWORD

	B	W		Z	A		A
L	I	L	O		U	R	B	A	N
	G	R		L		S		D
L	O	C	K	O	U	T		G
	T	O	T	S		A	G	R	A
D	R	O	O	L		B	O	A	S
	Y		P	O	I	S	O	N	S

FUTOSHIKI

2	3	1
1	2	3
3	1	2

SMALL CHANGE

1 Slipper, Sandal, Clog,
Mule, Boot 2 Axe, Drill,
Hammer, Saw, Clamp
3 Four, Fifty, Nine, One,
Eight 4 Judge, Chef, Vet,
Pilot, Cleaner 5 Rain,
Shower, Snow, Hail, Sleet

WORKOUT 60

NUMBER JIG

1 383 2 927 3 7352 4 4461

CODEWORDS

1 Hen 2 Hare 3 Otter (9=T)
4 Stoat 5 Hornet

FOUR BY FOUR

F	U	N	K
A	R	E	A
I	D	O	L
R	U	N	E

SOLUTIONS

WORKOUT 61

IN AND OUT
Sort (- P), cheat (+ E),
chart (+ R),   them (- R),
eyrie (+ Y) **PERRY**
Camp (+ M), whet (- A),
roué (- S), course (+ O),
chat (- N) **MASON**

FOUR BY FOUR

B	A	L	E
E	X	I	T
A	L	E	C
M	E	S	H

SPLITS
1 Clingfilm **2** Interview
3 Furniture **4** Hairspray
5 Turquoise

WORKOUT 62

MINI JIGSAW
Cyprus, Poland, Turkey
Norway, France, Canada

KILLER SUDOKU

2	9	6	5	7	3	1	4	8
1	5	4	9	8	6	7	2	3
8	3	7	1	2	4	9	6	5
6	1	8	4	3	9	5	7	2
3	7	9	2	1	5	6	8	4
5	4	2	7	6	8	3	9	1
4	6	1	3	9	2	8	5	7
9	2	3	8	5	7	4	1	6
7	8	5	6	4	1	2	3	9

WORKOUT 63

INITIALS
1 Hundreds and thousands
2 *Keeping Up Appearances*
3 *Are You Lonesome Tonight?*
4 *Raiders of the Lost Ark*
5 Bull in a china shop

MISSING LINK
1 Wave **2** Nail **3** Mark
4 High **5** Foot. The
constellation is **VIRGO**

FIX SIX

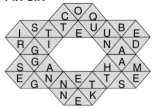

WORKOUT 64

WILD WORDS
1 You're under arrest **2** Forever
3 Cash in hand **4** No-one

ELIMINATION
Gemstones – Amber,
Diamond, Jade, Jet, Opal.
DRAW – Attract, Pull, Raffle,
Sketch, Tie.
BREAD – Crumb, Line,
Sauce, Stick, Winner.
Parts of the face – Brow,
Cheek, Chin, Lip, Nose.
Leftover phrase:
BRASS BAND

COPYCATS
1 Wrong **2** Elver **3** Upright
4 4297 (4th, 1st, 3rd and
2nd digits) **5** Milk

WORKOUT 65

WORDSEARCH

VOWEL PLAY
1 Silk **2** Denim **3** Wool **4** Rayon
5 Tweed **6** Paisley **7** Plaid
8 Linen **9** Angora **10** Suede

CELL BLOCKS

3		1		2
2	5			
			8	
3			4	
	3			3
			2	

WORKOUT 66

SUDOKU

1	4	3	2
2	3	4	1
4	1	2	3
3	2	1	4

1	2	4	3
3	4	1	2
2	1	3	4
4	3	2	1

1	4	2	3
2	3	1	4
4	1	3	2
3	2	4	1

ADD UP
1 37
2 35
3 46

WORKOUT 67

CODEWORD

SPOT THE SUM
1 22 (15+7) **2** 29 (18+11)
3 30 (18+12) **4** 35 (29+6)

WORKOUT 68

SCRAMBLE
1 Peru **2** Wales
3 Poland **4** Germany
5 Algeria **6** Thailand
7 Barbados **8** Cameroon

TENNIS MATCH
Photograph 4

WORKOUT 69

UTOSHIKI

ETTER SEQUENCE

M (+3) **2** P (-2) **3** T
5, -4, -3...) **4** O (alternate
, +1) **5** J (January,
ebruary...)

ISAVOWEL

WORKOUT 70

ITWORD

ig

ET SQUARE

9	+	6	÷	3
-		×		+
2	×	5	−	1
+		−		×
7	+	8	−	4

WORKOUT 71

PATHFINDER

WOOD, GREEN, UMBRELLA, BAG, HANDICAP, PITCH, SWING, HOLE, ROUND, FAIRWAY, HAZARD, ROUGH, FORE, ALBATROSS, EAGLE, GOLF, BIRDIE, FLAG, WEDGE, RYDER CUP, CADDY, BUNKER

PAIRS

Black market, hot dog, coffee break, day school, driving licence, English breakfast, French dressing, Green Party, head start, spoon-feed, tablecloth, trick cyclist

STAIRS and TIRED yield DIRE STRAITS

WORKOUT 72

HONEYCOMB

1 Far off **2** Ransom **3** Starve
4 Intend **5** Stroll **6** Malice
7 Common **8** Coward **9** Noodle
10&11 Norman Lamont

SUDOKU

2	1	4	9	6	7	5	3	8
9	3	6	1	8	5	4	7	2
7	5	8	2	3	4	6	1	9
3	7	1	4	5	8	2	9	6
5	8	9	6	1	2	3	4	7
4	6	2	3	7	9	1	8	5
1	2	3	8	9	6	7	5	4
6	9	5	7	4	1	8	2	3
8	4	7	5	2	3	9	6	1

MOBILE CODE

1 Oak **2** Pine **3** Cedar **4** Birch
5 Willow **6** Acacia

WORKOUT 73

WORD BUILDER

Reign, Grime, Arena, Miner, Anger, Grain, German, Remain, Marina, Armani, Margin, Mirage, Manager, Earring, Marriage, Margarine

WORDSEARCH

OPPOSITES ATTRACT

1 Sour/Sweet **2** Loose/Tight
3 Strong/Weak **4** Entrance/
Exit **5** Cheap/Expensive

WORKOUT 74

MEMORY QUIZ

1 Fe **2** Four **3** No,
it's supersede **4** The right
5 Yellow **6** V

SMART SUMS

1 4 (8-4) **2** 6 (30÷5) **3** 20
(4x5) **4** 54 (60-6) **5** 67 (64+3)

KAKURO

1	3		4	6	1	2	
2	1	5	9	8	3	6	4	7
	1	7	9	2		8	9

SOLUTIONS

WORKOUT 75
ARROWORD

S	T		C		S	
T	O	W	R	O	P	E	V
A		O		M	I	N	C	E
A	R	C		P	E	A	L	S
R	A	D	I	O		T	A	T
K	Y	L	E		S	N	O	R	E
	M	E	L	T		R	E	D

STAIRCASE
Strauss, Mahler, Elgar, Britten, Dvorak, Rossini, Glinka.
The "staircase" reveals:
SMETANA

SMALL CHANGE
1 Large, Big, Vast, Whopping, Massive **2** Helmet, Pump, Bike, Ride, Pedal **3** Ramble, March, Walk, Strut, Hike **4** Steam, Cook, Poach, Simmer, Fry

WORKOUT 76
NUMBER JIG
1 259 **2** 217 **3** 9464 **4** 3517

SPLITS
1 Partridge **2** Something
3 Quarterly **4** Carthorse
5 Bamboozle

FOUR BY FOUR

B	O	L	T
A	R	E	A
R	A	S	P
E	L	S	E

WORKOUT 77
NINERS
Chemistry, labyrinth, apartment, numerical
The left-hand column gives **CLAN**.

ALL FOURS

C	O	R	K
A	M	E	N
R	I	L	E
S	T	Y	E

BOX WISE
1 Cou **2** Rai **3** Sin **4** Ful **5** Lad
6 Led **7** Fil **8** Thy **9** Ger **10** Bil
11 Let **12** Low

WORKOUT 78
MINI JIGSAW
Monkey, Rabbit, Jaguar
Ferret, Donkey, Badger

KILLER SUDOKU

8	4	7	3	9	6	5	2	1
5	3	2	7	1	4	6	8	9
9	6	1	2	8	5	3	7	4
4	2	6	9	3	8	1	5	7
1	9	5	4	7	2	8	3	6
3	7	8	6	5	1	9	4	2
7	1	4	5	6	3	2	9	8
2	8	3	1	4	9	7	6	5
6	5	9	8	2	7	4	1	3

WORKOUT 79
FUTOSHIKI

3	1	2
1	2	3
2	3	1

3	2	1
2	1	3
1	3	2

2	3	1
1	2	3
3	1	2

WORD BUILDER
Apron, Prong, Groan, Spine, Orange, Ignore, Senior, Pigeon, Parson, Rope in, Sponger, Open-air, Iron Age, Searing, Organise, Singapore

WORKOUT 80
FARE'S FAIR

	R	A	Y	S
P	A	N	E	
S	I	D	E	
C	O	U	R	T
	D	E	W	
S	A	W		

SPLITS
1 Underwear **2** Evergreen
3 Community **4** Athletics
5 Miniature

WORKOUT 81
LOGICAL
Tom, Lake District, Chocolate
Dick, Peak District, Tea bags
Harry, Yorkshire Dales, Brandy

CELL BLOCKS

	2			4	
1		3			2
	2		4		
	3			3	
		2			
	6				4

WORKOUT 82
SUDOKU

4	3	1	2
1	2	4	3
2	4	3	1
3	1	2	4

1	3	4	2
4	2	1	3
2	1	3	4
3	4	2	1

2	3	4	1
4	1	3	2
1	4	2	3
3	2	1	4

WORDSEARCH

P	Y	E	K	C	O	J
E	U	T	S	R	B	R
L	P	R	U	Z	E	E
D	J	O	R	T	W	I
D	E	T	N	I	N	N
A	A	A	C	H	T	S
S	C	J	U	M	P	S

C	K	N	U	R	T	K
O	V	B	L	I	B	N
F	B	O	X	A	X	E
F	C	A	S	K	E	T
E	C	K	J	U	O	A
R	E	P	M	A	H	R
T	A	Q	E	T	M	C

L	W	P	A	G	X	A
I	A	E	P	V	L	J
Z	L	C	H	M	E	F
A	N	A	O	S	Z	B
R	S	N	W	Y	A	I
B	D	H	P	K	H	C
M	O	N	K	E	Y	Z

WORKOUT 83
CODEWORD

	K		Y		M		F		R		A	
S	A	M	O	S	A		U	N	E	A	S	Y
	R		G		N	I	L		T		C	
L	A	V	I	S	H		L	O	O	M	E	D
	T				O		Y		R		N	
B	E	A	S	T	L	Y		S	T	U	D	Y
			O		E		O		E			
B	U	S	B	Y		P	R	U	D	I	S	H
	N		E		J		B				E	
F	I	E	R	C	E		I	N	S	T	I	L
	Q				W	E	T		A		Z	
Q	U	I	N	C	E		E	X	I	T	E	D
	E				D		D		D		D	

SO COMPLETE

Wild,	wide,	idle	D
Warn,	wren,	wear	R
Dear,	moat,	alas	A
Café,	ford,	leaf	F
Test,	mate,	sett	T

WORKOUT 84

POT THE SUM

21 (14+7) **3** 36 (32+4)
24 (15+9) **4** 33 (28+5)

PIECEWORD

WORKOUT 85

MIX-UP

(Yellow) SUBMARINE
(Blue) VELVET **3** (Yellow)
IVER **4** (Yellow) ROLLS
OYCE **5** (Blue) HOTEL
(Blue) HAWAII **7** (Blue)
MOON **8** (Yellow)
RICK ROAD **9** (Yellow)
OSE OF TEXAS **10** (Blue)
UEDE SHOES

FOUR BY FOUR

WORKOUT 86

ITWORD

WARPAINT
PROPELLED
AMPERED
PROPOSER
BALANCING
SCOLDING

agabond

SIX PACK

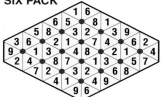

WORKOUT 87

PATHFINDER

THE BOYFRIEND, CHICAGO,
MAME, INTO THE WOODS, FUNNY
FACE, MAMMA MIA, GREASE,
SWEET CHARITY, THE LION KING,
MARY POPPINS, BRIGADOON,
GODSPELL, OKLAHOMA, HAIR

SOUNDALIKES

1 Knew/new **2** Stile/style
3 I'll/aisle **4** Mussels/muscles

COPYCATS

1 Duck **2** 169 (square numbers)
3 Dame (replace 3rd letter with
next one in the alphabet) **4** Bow

WORKOUT 88

BUZZ OFF

1 and 6

SUDOKU

9	4	8	2	6	1	3	5	7
2	1	5	8	7	3	4	9	6
7	6	3	4	5	9	8	2	1
6	3	2	5	8	4	7	1	9
4	7	1	9	2	6	5	8	3
8	5	9	3	1	7	6	4	2
5	8	6	7	9	2	1	3	4
3	2	7	1	4	5	9	6	8
1	9	4	6	3	8	2	7	5

SPLITS

1 Concerned **2** Machinist
3 Beautiful **4** Boulevard
5 Pageantry

WORKOUT 89

LETTERSETS

S	A	L	A	D		O	R	B
A	C	E		E	L	F		E
G	U	E	S	S		F	A	N
	T		A	P	T			D
Y	E	S	T	E	R	D	A	Y
E		E	R	A		R		
A	R	T		A	M	I	S	S
R		O	P	T		C	O	O
N	E	W		E	V	E	N	T

WORDSEARCH

FUTOSHIKI

1	3	2
2	1	3
3	2	1

WORKOUT 90

SMART SUMS

1 36 (4+32) **2** 1396
(1488-92) **3** 52 (20+32)
4 48 (3x16) **5** 33 (51-18)

SMALL CHANGE

1 Snap, Bridge, Rummy,
Poker, Whist **2** Fairy, Imp,
Troll, Elf, Peri **3** Bake,
Roast, Grill, Stew, Poach
4 Deacon, Dean, Verger,
Beadle, Pastor

KAKURO

3	1		4	6	1	2	
1	2	5	9	8	3	6	4	7
		1	7	9	2		8	9

SOLUTIONS

WORKOUT 91
ARROWORD

	S	D	K	S	A
S	H	O	E	I	D	L	E	S
I		M		L		Y	H
U	N	G	O	D	L	Y		W
	D	U	N	E		M	E	A	D
M	I	N	I	M		C	A	N	E
G		C	O	W	A	R	D	S

VOWEL PLAY
1 Judo **2** Polo **3** Aerobics
4 Karate **5** Boxing **6** Diving
7 Rugby **8** Tennis **9** Archery
10 Football

TWO OF A KIND
1 Convent/nunnery
2 Consider/deliberate
3 Result/upshot **4** Fuming/
ireful **5** Giggling/laughter

WORKOUT 92
FIX SIX

MOBILE CODE
1 Derby **2** Truro **3** Exeter
4 Ipswich **5** Taunton

INITIALS
1 The Virgin Queen **2** *To Kill
a Mockingbird* **3** *The Winner
Takes it All* **4** *Kind Hearts and
Coronets* **5** Neither a borrower
nor a lender be

WORKOUT 93
MIND THE GAP
Despair, Alarmed, Gnasher,
Steamer, Enforce, Educate,
Timpani, Haulier.

The shaded word is:
PASTRAMI

FOUR BY FOUR

B	O	A	T
E	M	I	R
C	E	D	E
K	N	E	E

BOX WISE
1 Mar **2** Pur **3** Lin **4** Ger
5 Gey **6** Ser **7** Bil **8** Low
9 Ver **10** Bal **11** Let **12** Sam

WORKOUT 94
MINI JIGSAW
Boxing, Shinty, Tennis
Squash, Hockey, Skiing

KILLER SUDOKU

6	2	7	3	5	8	4	1	9
8	1	3	4	9	2	7	6	5
9	4	5	7	1	6	3	8	2
1	6	9	5	7	3	8	2	4
3	7	8	2	4	1	5	9	6
4	5	2	6	8	9	1	7	3
2	8	1	9	3	5	6	4	7
5	9	4	1	6	7	2	3	8
7	3	6	8	2	4	9	5	1

WORKOUT 95
WORD BUILDER
Peace, Nacre, Erect, Caper,
Pecan, Crate, Recent,
Career, Carpet, Create,
Centre, Nectar, Terrace,
Reenact, Retrace, Carpenter

NUMBER JIG
1 897 **2** 435 **3** 5768 **4** 1212

WORKOUT 96
IN AND OUT
Steam (+ T), cream (+ E),
tough (- R), Spain (- R),
tansy (+ Y) **TERRY**

Town (+ W), tut (- A), ideal
(+ I), sleigh (- T), crate (- E)
WAITE

SET SQUARE

9	+	6	÷	3
+		×		×
1	+	4	÷	5
×		−		−
2	×	7	−	8

ELIMINATION
Sand ___ – Bag, Castle,
Paper, Pit, Storm
Synonyms of Chasm –
Abyss, Crater, Crevasse,
Gorge, Ravine
Trees – Ash, Banyan,
Beech, Sycamore, Willow
Aircraft – Airship, Balloon,
Glider, Helicopter, Jet.
Remaining: **CLIFFHANGER**

WORKOUT 97
WORDSEARCH

SPLITS
1 Miserable **2** Hysterics
3 Parachute **4** Essential
5 Starboard

CELL BLOCKS

			3		
					4
		5			
4	4				
				8	2
4			2		

SOLUTIONS

WORKOUT 98

SUDOKU

4	1	2	3
3	2	4	1
1	4	3	2
2	3	1	4

2	4	1	3
1	3	2	4
3	2	4	1
4	1	3	2

3	2	4	1
4	1	3	2
2	4	1	3
1	3	2	4

ADD UP
1 44
2 48
3 36

WORKOUT 99

CODEWORD

D D B S J T
AZEBO HEEDED
Y W N R T N
TAY SKITTISH
I A L I E
MPERIALISM
E A O G
PROVIDENTLY
S P O E U
SQUIRREL FACT
U E T V A O
AUCHE EXCESS
D E X D E E

COPYCATS
0.4 **2** Crave **3** Virtue
Pearl **5** Tray

WORKOUT 100

SHAPE UP

CPEBHEBNPF
AOUAAPAEUU
MPSLRPRWTL
OLTHRINHNH
EAOAONEAEA
NRNMWGTMYM

WORKOUT 101

CODEWORDS
Tea **2** Wine **3** Cider
Soda **5** Retsina

SCRAMBLE
1 Cape **2** Dale **3** West
4 Shore **5** Desert **6** Stream
7 Coppice **8** Estuary
9 Snowcap **10** Everglades

PYRAMID
1 A **2** Ta **3** Sat **4** Tans
5 Saint **6** Tisane **7** Estonia
8 Obeisant **9** Baritones

WORKOUT 102

FITWORD

HAVOC BUY
E O L A E
RAW ONSET
E W M I
BIANNUAL
Y R T A
STAFFING
I W U E
DROSS KIN
E R E O C
ASK DAILY

Gargle

ALPHA-BEATER

C F FEZ J
HEAVE ALLOT
I B L P K
CALLOW ICED
E N Q I
MODE JUTTED
N G A R A
HYENA ROUST
X PET S E

WORKOUT 103

PATHFINDER

ANEMONE, NERINE, TULIP, SNOWDROP,
GLADIOLUS, IXIA, BEGONIA, DAFFODIL,
DAHLIA, LILY, BLUEBELL, ALLIUM,
ACONITE, SCILLA, CROCUS, JONQUIL,
FREESIA, MONTBRETIA

FUTOSHIKI

3	1	2
2	3	1
1	2	3

SMALL CHANGE
1 Ferry, Tug, Junk,
Canoe, Tanker **2** Dupe,
Trick, Con, Cheat, Gull
3 Snow, Frost, Hail, Rain,
Sleet **4** Prawn, Crab,
Clam, Winkle, Cockle

WORKOUT 104

DISAVOWEL

OBOE PLURAL
ROUE A NOVA
ASTRAL DAIS
LURID HORDE
NEED O I R
E A TWINE
ROCOCO OGRE
ASHLAR N E
I DRIEST B
RENEGE OVA
R ROSARY A

SUDOKU

1	9	7	8	3	2	4	6	5
8	3	4	7	6	5	2	1	9
5	6	2	4	9	1	7	3	8
6	8	5	2	1	3	9	4	7
4	2	3	9	5	7	6	8	1
9	7	1	6	4	8	3	5	2
2	4	9	5	8	6	1	7	3
3	5	6	1	7	9	8	2	4
7	1	8	3	2	4	5	9	6

THREE IN ONE
1 Bill **2** Chair **3** Common
4 Wear **5** Spell

SOLUTIONS

WORKOUT 105

MINI FIT
1 Tut **2** Flu **3** Ally **4** Corn

WORDSEARCH

CODEWORD
1 Sea **2** Crab **3** Coast (9=T)
4 Resort **5** Bathers

WORKOUT 106

MIND THE GAP
1 Tin **2** Par **3** Hat **4** The **5** Pat

STAIRCASE
Georgia, Imogen, Kelly,
Pauline, Claire, Amelia, Lillian.
The word is: **GILLIAN**

KAKURO
	9	3	1	8		2	1
9	8	5	1	2	7	4	6	3
7	9		6	4	9	8	

WORKOUT 107

ARROWORD

VOWEL PLAY
1 Pug **2** Boxer **3** Corgi **4** Beagle
5 Collie **6** Lurcher **7** Samoyed
8 Alsatian **9** Retriever **10** Terrier

CODEWORDS
1 Mike **2** Lima **3** Echo
4 Sierra **5** Charlie

WORKOUT 108

WORDSEARCH

LETTER SEQUENCE
1 T (+2, +4, +3, repeated)
2 F (+13, -11, +13, -10, +13,
-9 etc) **3** T (alternate in pairs
+1, +2; +1, +3; +1, +4 etc)
4 V (initial letters of rainbow
colors) **5** E (initials of British
monarchs from George IV
onwards). Well done if you
got 4 and 5

FOUR BY FOUR

WORKOUT 109

PAIRS
Backgammon, beanpole,
birthstone, doormat,
front-runner, market day,
mountain bike, penny black,
Royal Marine, string vest,
table manners, visiting card
Safe recipe – Fire escape

SPLITS
1 Barricade **2** Enunciate
3 Ingenious **4** Featuring
5 Hideously

BOX WISE
1 But **2** Car **3** Ton **4** Ing
5 Par **6** Rot **7** Est **8** Eem
9 Ten **10** Don **11** Ate **12** Key

WORKOUT 110

MINI JIGSAW
Blazer, Kimono, Blouse
Jersey, Shorts, Anorak

SO COMPLETE
Draw,	dawn,	swan	W
White,	ashen,	hoist	H
Pain,	shift,	like	I
Morass,	caress,	chase	S
King,	wink,	skin	K

WORKOUT 111

WORD BUILDER
Pslam, Prams, Slump, Prism,
Maria, Mails, Plums, Murals,
Plasma, Salami, Primal,
Alarms, Samurai, Impalas,
Marsupial

TAKE FIVE

WORKOUT 112

WILD WORDS
1 Lion King **2** Six of one,
half-a-dozen of the other
3 Crossroads **4** Caught in
the act

MISSING LINK
1 Cold **2** Knee **3** Time
4 Book **5** Land – Lemon

ELIMINATION
Body parts – Café (face),
Earth (heart), Viler (liver),
Keen (knee), Lose (sole)

Green things – Emerald,
Grass, Jade, Lime, Olive

OIL – Drum, Rig, Slick, Skin,
Well

Square numbers – Four, Nine,
One, Sixteen, Twenty-five

Leftover word: **TWO-STEP**

SOLUTIONS

WORKOUT 113

MINI FIT
Ode **2** Pat

CELL BLOCKS

	4		2	
3			4	
2	2	2		
				3
3	3			3
	4			1

WORKOUT 114

SUDOKU

3	1	4	2
2	4	3	1
1	3	2	4
4	2	1	3

3	2	1	4
1	4	2	3
2	3	4	1
4	1	3	2

2	4	3	1
3	1	2	4
4	3	1	2
1	2	4	3

ADD UP
1 50
2 39
3 60

WORKOUT 115

CODEWORD

SPOT THE SUM
1 23 (9+14) **2** 20 (4+16)
3 18 (4+14) **4** 32 (13+19)

WORKOUT 116

NINERS
Blackmail, replenish, automaton, yesterday
The left-hand column gives
BRAY.

MANE LINE
Photograph 1

WORKOUT 117

MOBILE CODE
1 Cole **2** Clooney **3** Formby
4 Foreman **5** Michael **6** Peppard

LOGICAL
Curly, 5 years, football, West
Hambo, 3 years, truffle hunting, South
Trotter, 4 years, mudbath, North

HONEYCOMB
1 Thrice **2** Docile **3** Nursed
4 Almost **5** Oracle **6** Fleece
7 Confer **8** Grouse **9** Raisin
10&11 Second fiddle

WORKOUT 118

FITWORD

	F	I	R	M	E	S	T
T		L		A		T	U
S	I	L	L	I	N	E	S	S
A		M		E		E	
R	U	M	P		B	R	E	D
		A			E		
L	U	G	E		E	D	G	Y
O		I		K		O	
A	S	C	E	N	D	I	N	G
D		A		O		N	A
	S	L	O	W	I	N	G

Dew

SET SQUARE

1	+	6	×	4
+		×		÷
7	+	9	÷	2
÷		÷		+
8	+	3	−	5

WORKOUT 119

PATHFINDER

MAORI, SWEDISH, HINDI, FRENCH, KASHMIRI, WELSH, ENGLISH, RUSSIAN, CZECH, URDU, JAPANESE, ROMANY, SWAHILI, TURKISH, ICELANDIC, POLISH, DUTCH, PUNJABI, SPANISH

NUMBER JIG
1 284 **2** 153 **3** 6621

ALPHA-FIT

WORKOUT 120

PYRAMID
1 E **2** Re **3** Ire **4** Erin
5 Miner **6** Remain **7** Minaret
8 Terminal **9** Tramlines

SUDOKU

4	5	7	3	6	8	9	1	2
6	2	8	5	9	1	7	4	3
1	3	9	2	4	7	6	8	5
9	7	5	4	8	2	3	6	1
8	1	6	9	5	3	2	7	4
3	4	2	1	7	6	8	5	9
7	9	4	8	2	5	1	3	6
2	8	1	6	3	4	5	9	7
5	6	3	7	1	9	4	2	8

STAIRCASE
Yellow, Darling, Danube, Ganges, Trent, Zambezi, Garonne. The "staircase" reveals: **YANGTZE**

SOLUTIONS

WORKOUT 121

SUDOKU

1	2	4	3
4	3	2	1
3	4	1	2
2	1	3	4

2	4	3	1
1	3	2	4
3	1	4	2
4	2	1	3

3	1	4	2
2	4	3	1
1	3	2	4
4	2	1	3

WORDSEARCH

```
C L A R I N E T  I
O B O E E D G C R
B N Y K N R L U B
E A A D O U O A R
T C N I H M S T E
U A E J P S M R H
L N I L O I V M T
F Z N O L W E M I
S J N V Y O P P Z
P R A H X B X E H
G U I T A R F U T
```

FOUR BY FOUR

```
W I R E
E D E N
L E A D
D A D S
```

WORKOUT 122

SMART SUMS

1 2 (14÷7) **2** 10 (6+4) **3** 16 (4x4)
4 202 (204-2) **5** 72 (24x3)

OPPOSITES ATTRACT

1 Broke/loaded **2** Separate/
together **3** Private/public
4 Correct/improper

KAKURO

		2	4	1	6		8	9
2	1	6	9	3	8	5	4	7
1	3		7	2	9	1		

WORKOUT 123

ARROWORD

```
  B O   F   T
  I M P E R F E C T
  S   T   E R A   A
Y E S     T O T A L
  C L A M   L I V E
S T O P   S I M O N
  P T O   C E N T
```

SPLITS

1 Essayists **2** Fireproof
3 Scholarly **4** Runaround
5 Dexterity

LOGICAL

Sanjeev, Gold, Long jump
Chuck, Silver, 100m
Russell, Bronze, Discus

WORKOUT 124

CAKE BAKE

3 and 4

TWO OF A KIND

1 Absolute/complete
2 Magnate/tycoon
3 Enormity/vastness
4 Constant/permanent
5 Champion/victor

STAIRCASE

Cradle, Tallboy, Table,
Divan, Bench, Rocker,
Whatnot.

The furniture item is:

CABINET

WORKOUT 125

FARE'S FAIR

```
R I G H T
  T I M E
S A N E
R E I G N
I D L E
F A R E
```

FUTOSHIKI

```
1 3 2
2 1 3
3 2 1
```

WORKOUT 126

MINI JIGSAW

Sorbet, Mousse, Trifle
Yogurt, Sundae, Gateau

KILLER SUDOKU

9	3	4	6	7	5	8	1	2
1	8	5	2	9	3	4	7	6
7	6	2	1	4	8	5	3	9
5	1	3	8	6	2	7	9	4
4	2	6	7	3	9	1	5	8
8	9	7	4	5	1	6	2	3
6	4	9	5	2	7	3	8	1
2	5	8	3	1	6	9	4	7
3	7	1	9	8	4	2	6	5

WORKOUT 127

WORD BUILDER

Antic, Dance, Acute, Enact,
Ocean, Tonic, Canoe,
Toucan, Action, Deacon,
Induce, Octane, Noticed,
Counted, Conduit, Cautioned,
Auctioned, Education

WORDSEARCH

```
I S N G R P S
D I T C N R M
Q U E E N I O
J Q K O K N K
V R R E Q C F
Y A L R A E H
B M B U D P X
```

```
O L L E T O H
N N C X T T T
O E Z D E O F
R M U B S A A
M R C C K D U
A A A G M I S
M C I J H A T
```

```
C O O L G I I
N O I S N A M
T M T L S H E
Y A W T C N S
V I L L A X A
O E J F D G K
B E D S I T E
```

WORKOUT 128

NINERS
Recollect, orphanage,
mincemeat, eastwards
The left-hand column gives
ROME.

SET SQUARE

7	×	8	÷	4
+		−		+
9	+	1	−	5
−		×		÷
6	×	2	−	3

ELIMINATION
Reindeer – Comet, Cupid,
Dasher, Dancer, Vixen.
___ Ball – Hand, Odd, Pin,
Punch, Screw.
Egg-layers – Bee, Goose,
Platypus, Salmon, Turtle.
Dances – Foxtrot, Jive,
Samba, Tango, Waltz.
Leftover phrase:
PRINCIPAL BOY

WORKOUT 129

WORDSEARCH

PAIRS
Armrest, borderline, bow
tie, breakneck, chairwoman,
cricket pitch, downmarket,
French window, garden
centre, outfield, scarlet
fever, spread eagle

GERM and VALIANT yield
MALT VINEGAR

CELL BLOCKS

		6	
6	6		6
			6
	6		

WORKOUT 130

SUDOKU

1	4	3	2
3	2	4	1
4	1	2	3
2	3	1	4

ADD UP
1 36
2 48
3 31

4	1	3	2
3	2	1	4
1	4	2	3
2	3	4	1

4	2	1	3
1	3	4	2
2	1	3	4
3	4	2	1

WORKOUT 131

CODEWORD

1 Green 2 Left 3 Broccoli
4 Left 5 £5 note – the Queen
and Elizabeth Fry 6 Red

MASYU

WORKOUT 132

SPLITS
1 Periphery 2 Childcare
3 Mutineers 4 Menagerie
5 Weathered

BABY FACE
Photograph 3

WORKOUT 133

NUMBER SEQUENCE
1 91 (+(2x2), +(3x3) etc)
2 30 (+8,-2,+9,-3, +10,-4
etc) 3 6 (this one's tricky –
it's the number of letters in
the names of the months,
starting with January)
4 58 (sum of the numbers
1 and 3 places before)
5 70 (+(2x2),+(2x2x2) etc)

INITIALS
1 King Kong 2 *Oranges
and Lemons* 3 The Lake
District 4 The Leaning
Tower of Pisa 5 *Joseph
and the Amazing
Technicolor Dreamcoat*

PYRAMID
1 E 2 Te 3 Set 4 Rest
5 Steer 6 Teaser 7 Serrate
8 Traverse 9 Harvester

WORKOUT 134

FITWORD

C	O	C	O	A		B	U	T
A		R		L		A		A
T	E	A		S	I	D	E	S
T		M		O				T
Y	I	P	S		S	T	A	Y
		E			I			
R	O	D	E		S	N	O	B
O			R		T			A
G	U	S	T	O		I	T	S
U		O		O		N		I
E	B	B		M	O	G	U	L

Farce

WORD BUILDER
Alien, Agent, Navel, Angel,
Naïve, Angle, Native,
Ignite, Genial, Invite,
Tangle, Entail, Leaving,
Vintage, Tailing, Veiling,
Vigilant, Valeting, Vigilante

SOLUTIONS

WORKOUT 135
PATHFINDER

FARFALLE, FUSILLI, MACARONI, NOODLES, LASAGNE, RADIATORE, RIGATONI, TAGLIATELLE, CONCHIGLIE, LINGUINE, PASTA, SPAGHETTI, VERMICELLI, GEMELLI, RAVIOLI

NUMBER JIG
1 121 **2** 942 **3** 3689

LEAF ALONE

WORKOUT 136
SPOT THE SUM
1 22 (15+7) **2** 29 (18+11) **3** 30 (18+12) **4** 35 (29+6)

SUDOKU

1	8	5	6	2	7	4	3	9
4	7	9	3	8	5	1	6	2
3	2	6	4	1	9	7	8	5
7	3	2	9	5	1	6	4	8
5	9	1	8	4	6	3	2	7
6	4	8	2	7	3	9	5	1
9	5	4	7	6	2	8	1	3
8	1	7	5	3	4	2	9	6
2	6	3	1	9	8	5	7	4

SCRAMBLE
1 Leo **2** Aries **3** Orion **4** Plough **5** Pisces **6** Great bear **7** Andromeda **8** Capricorn

WORKOUT 137
SIX PACK

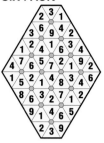

WORD SEARCH

SMART SUMS
1 32 (144-112) **2** 150 (366-216) **3** 48 (4x12) **4** 27 (6+21) **5** 81 (9x9)

WORKOUT 138
COPYCATS
1 Clarinet **2** Gape (1st and 3rd letter pattern: 1 lower and 2 lower) **3** Asia **4** Gas

KAKURO

WORKOUT 139
ARROWORD

	N		I	G		A
S	C	R	I	P	T	U	R	E	S
	R		G		V		O		K
B	A	T	H	S		C	U	T	
N	O	T	E	P	A	P	E	R	
B	E	G	I	N		S	I	L	O
	S	E	D	A	T	E	L	Y	

VOWEL PLAY
1 Bay **2** Mace **3** Mint **4** Sage **5** Anise **6** Borage **7** Aniseed **8** Oregano **9** Rosemary **10** Turmeric

SMALL CHANGE
1 Hall, Loft, Chamber, Suite Cellar **2** Bloom, Stalk, Petal Leaf, Seed **3** Sole, Tyne, Dogger, Dover, Bailey **4** Hearing, Touch, Sight, Taste, Smell **5** Joy, Bliss, Glee, Rapture, Exultation

WORKOUT 140
FIX SIX

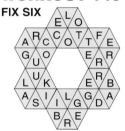

MOBILE CODE
1 Sum **2** Mean **3** Root **4** Value **5** Matrix

FOUR BY FOUR

B	O	O	K
A	C	M	E
W	H	E	Y
L	E	N	S

WORKOUT 141
SET SQUARE

8	−	4	×	9
−		×		÷
1	×	6	÷	3
×		÷		+
5	×	2	−	7

TAKE FIVE

T	A	B	L	E
A		R		B
B	R	A	V	O
L		V		N
E	B	O	N	Y

MIND THE GAP
Secured, Deviant, Deplete, Trouser, Spangle, Maidens, Hoaxers, Reproof.

The shaded word is: **CALENDAR**

WORKOUT 142
MINI JIGSAW
Carafe, Scales, Cooker, Fridge, Juicer, Larder

⬛LLER SUDOKU

9	1	5	7	2	3	6	4	8
8	2	4	6	1	5	9	3	7
6	3	7	9	4	8	1	2	5
5	4	8	3	6	9	2	7	1
7	9	2	4	5	1	8	6	3
1	6	3	8	7	2	5	9	4
3	5	6	1	9	4	7	8	2
4	7	1	2	8	6	3	5	9
2	8	9	5	3	7	4	1	6

WORKOUT 143
MINI FIT
1 Awn 2 Lap 3 Wash 4 Apse

DOMINOES
1 Paella 2 Lychee 3 Cashew
4 Cassis 5 Raisin 6 Panini

WORKOUT 144
STEP RIDDLE
Limes, Times, Tomes, Tones, Tongs, Tonga

BOX WISE
1 Sto 2 War 3 Red 4 Der
5 Gar 6 Den 7 Mal 8 Let
9 Tal 10 Ent 11 Ice 12 Rap

SOUNDALIKES
1 Ruff/rough 2 Main/mein
3 Brewed/brood 4 Whine/wine

WORKOUT 145
WORDSEARCH

B	H	L	E	G	A	B		C	R	E	A	M	Y	O
F	L	B	L	T	L	N		Y	H	Q	K	O	R	X
A	C	O	T	O	A	S		E	C	E	G	L	F	T
D	Q	I	O	K	R	R		H	D	U	E	H	I	Z
L	P	W	U	M	F	P		W	R	K	N	S	M	M
X	J	G	Z	M	E	O		T	W	P	G	V	E	I
I	E	D	V	Y	T	R		J	A	Y	U	B	E	L

SPLITS
1 Presenter 2 Porcelain
3 Coriander 4 Geography
5 Manifesto

CELL BLOCKS

WORKOUT 146
SUDOKU

4	3	1	2
1	2	4	3
3	1	2	4
2	4	3	1

4	3	2	1
2	1	4	3
3	2	1	4
1	4	3	2

3	4	1	2
1	2	4	3
4	3	2	1
2	1	3	4

ADD UP
1 31 2 36 3 41

WORKOUT 147
CODEWORD

I		K		S		U		F		B		K
G	U	N	R	U	N	N	E	R		E	W	E
N		I		C		P		E		Q		Y
O	P	T	I	C	A	L		E	X	U	D	E
R		I		U				E				D
E	L	F		N	I	G	H	T	C	A	P	
		L		C				E		T		
	F	O	O	T	W	E	A	R		H	O	D
A		U		N		R				I		
B	A	N	J	O		G	L	A	Z	I	N	G
O		C		A		A		P		T		E
V	I	E		S	O	G	G	I	N	E	S	S
E		D		T		E		N		M		T

THREE IN ONE
1 Case 2 Pen 3 Last 4 Jet
5 Hold

WORKOUT 148
SHAPE UP

L	B	B	T	G	T	B	F	S	B
O	O	R	U	A	R	O		E	A	O
A	A	O	R	L	I	O	D	N	W
F	T	G	B	O	L	T	O	D	L
E	E	U	A	S	B	E	R	A	E
R	R	E	N	H	Y	E	A	L	R

WORKOUT 149
FUTOSHIKI

1	3	4	2
2	1	3	4
4	2	1	3
3	4	2	1

CODEWORDS
1 Pea 2 Corn 3 Caper
4 Crisp 5 Scone

TOWN TO TOWN
DALSTON
1 Talons 2 Altos 3 Last
4 Sat 5 Teas 6 Hates
7 Thames
WEST HAM

WORKOUT 150
FITWORD

L	U	R	K		G	A	R	B
O		O			S		O	
B	E	S	E	E	C	H	E	D
E		T		M		E		Y
	T	I	P	P	I	N	G	
U			E			I		
	T	E	A	R	I	N	G	
A		X		O		O		F
S	U	P	E	R	S	T	A	R
T		A			E		A	
I	O	T	A		I	D	L	Y

Sarcastic

SPOT THE SUM
1 33 (14+19) 2 33 (12+21)
3 21 (3+18) 4 34 (6+28)

SOLUTIONS

WORKOUT 151
PATHFINDER

D	G	N	I	P	D	A	E	L	R	E
I	N	I	P	N	I	T	D	A	G	G
N	I	O	M	N	U	O	R	M	U	L
G	R	O	W	O	D	P	E	S	S	P
O	P	A	E	H	W	E	F	O	O	R
N	U	D	D	R	O	M	P	R	T	R
S	T	Y	C	A	O	R	U	S	C	E
N	E	R	H	A	L	L	S	P	E	V
N	A	O	V	L	A	B	I	L	R	E
S	P	L	E	L	B	R	E	N	E	N
R	E	V	R	Y	R	A	E	R	G	D

SUSPECT, REVEREND GREEN, LIBRARY, REVOLVER, SPANNER, HALL, BALLROOM, PROFESSOR PLUM, ROPE, WHODUNNIT, DAGGER, LEAD PIPING, DINING ROOM, WEAPON, STUDY, CARD

ADD UP
1 26 **2** 60 **3** 42

IN AND OUT
Dance (+ C), nice (- H), glean (+ A), claim (+ I), vie (- N) **CHAIN**
Roué (- S), pleat (+ T), shut (- O), spires (+ R), wave (- E) **STORE**

WORKOUT 152
COMPLETE WORKS

Rich	sham	bash	H
Shear	laver	amber	A
Drive	alive	avert	V
Strop	stout	choir	O
Price	click	cheat	C

SUDOKU

1	8	6	2	5	4	9	7	3
7	5	9	6	3	8	4	2	1
3	4	2	7	1	9	6	8	5
9	3	1	5	8	2	7	6	4
8	6	7	9	4	3	1	5	2
4	2	5	1	7	6	8	3	9
2	7	3	8	9	1	5	4	6
6	9	8	4	2	5	3	1	7
5	1	4	3	6	7	2	9	8

FOUR BY FOUR

C	O	W	S
A	B	E	T
S	O	L	E
H	E	L	P

WORKOUT 153
WORD BUILDER
Feast, Feats, Cafes, Feint, Facts, Faint, Fiesta, Fasten, Finest, Fiance, Infest, Facets, Fanciest, Fanatics, Fascinate

WORDSEARCH

A	K	A	S	N	A	H	D	V
D	I	O	B	A	L	T	I	A
N	J	H	R	Z	B	N	M	K
A	C	A	T	M	D	R	A	K
S	N	F	L	A	A	V	D	I
A	D	U	L	F	P	H	R	T
P	Q	O	H	C	R	L	A	W
I	O	A	U	B	A	E	S	L
B	I	R	Y	A	N	I	Z	X
U	R	J	H	E	C	I	R	N
Y	M	P	K	E	E	M	A	N

SPLITS
1 Demanding **2** Infringes **3** Digestive **4** Secretary **5** Crimplene

WORKOUT 154
SUDOKU

2	3	4	1
4	1	2	3
1	2	3	4
3	4	1	2

3	2	4	1
4	1	2	3
2	3	1	4
1	4	3	2

2	1	3	4
4	3	2	1
1	2	4	3
3	4	1	2

WILD WORDS
1 Jagged edge
2 I understand
3 Backbone
4 Rising damp
5 Round of applause

KAKURO

WORKOUT 155
ARROWORD

U	G	J	L	A
A	S	T	U	T	E	N	E	S	S
S	M	W	B	P
W	R	A	T	H	M	A	P
P	R	A	L	I	N	E	S
C	H	E	E	R	R	O	T	A
D	E	E	P	E	N	E	D

INITIALS
1 *All Creatures Great and Small* **2** Pickled onion **3** Sherlock Holmes and Dr Watson **4** *My Heart Will Go On* **5** *All's Well That Ends Well*

VOWEL PLAY
1 Noel **2** Carol **3** Reindeer **4** Bauble **5** Tree **6** Grotto **7** Elf **8** Santa **9** Wreath **10** Wenceslas

WORKOUT 156
ODD ONE OUT
Picture 4

SCRAMBLE
1 Etna **2** Sinai **3** Snowdon **4** Everest **5** McKinley **6** Matterhorn **7** Krakatoa **8** Kilimanjaro

FOUR BY FOUR

B	O	W	S
O	V	A	L
M	E	R	E
B	R	E	D

WORKOUT 157

NUMBER JIG

5	5	2	■	3	8	2	7	1
7	2	3	8	1	■	9	3	2
4	4	6	■	3	9	2	6	5
3	7	5	8	0	1	4	■	2
■	5	■	5	■	1	■	1	■
3	■	7	8	8	4	3	5	7
8	8	7	0	4	■	8	1	0
8	6	8	■	5	7	2	0	6
4	1	3	6	3	■	3	4	4

MIND THE GAP
■ Win **2** Arc **3** Sew **4** Get **5** Nab

MISSING LINK
■ Pace **2** Walk **3** Slow
4 Sour **5** Tide. The weather
feature is: **CLOUD**

WORKOUT 158

MINI JIGSAW
Palace, Church, Prison
Museum, Hostel, Garage

KILLER SUDOKU

5	4	7	8	6	1	2	9	3
6	1	2	3	9	4	7	8	5
9	8	3	5	2	7	6	1	4
2	5	8	4	1	9	3	7	6
3	6	1	2	7	8	4	5	9
7	9	4	6	5	3	1	2	8
1	7	6	9	4	5	8	3	2
4	3	9	1	8	2	5	6	7
8	2	5	7	3	6	9	4	1

WORKOUT 159

NUMBER JIG

7	■	8	1	4	9	5	■	4
9	1	4	2	■	3	5	1	6
1	2	2	0	■	5	5	2	2
3	3	3	■	1	3	5	3	1
■	9	■	1	4	9	■	6	■
1	8	5	3	1	■	1	7	4
7	7	5	5	■	2	1	8	3
7	6	9	8	■	5	6	9	8
1	■	6	1	2	9	3	■	0

Leftover number: **4523**

MINI FIT
1 Tin **2** Dog **3** Road **4** Claw

WORKOUT 160

ELIMINATION
Adverbs – Fast, Greedily,
Happily, Much, Well.

Young animals – Calf, Chick,
Kid, Lamb, Puppy.

Hats – Bowler, Cloche,
Mitre, Topper, Trilby.

SLEEP synonyms – Doze,
Kip, Nap, Slumber, Snooze.

Remaining: **HOTHEAD**

FARE'S FAIR

		S	H	O	R	E	
		L	Y	N	X		
			P	H	L	O	X
R	I	G	H	T			
		S	E	E	N		
B	A	N	D				

SET SQUARE

8	+	3	×	2
÷		+		×
4	+	9	−	5
×		÷		−
7	+	6	−	1

WORKOUT 161

WORDSEARCH

S	G	L	C	S	P	D		L	O	A	F	E	R	E
O	S	J	U	D	G	E		P	J	M	E	P	S	V
R	J	E	W	I	L	X		X	D	Y	U	B	M	O
Z	U	U	N	A	B	J		G	F	M	G	L	I	T
T	R	K	I	T	V	A		R	P	F	O	O	E	K
H	Y	R	M	E	I	Y		W	N	A	R	Q	L	E
F	T	K	C	O	D	W		H	L	Z	B	U	C	C

COPYCATS
1 Link (reverse word and
add K) **2** 7 (9 lower) **3** Sting
(weapon) **4** Mast (first letter
eight higher in the alphabet)
5 Breed (second vowel one
vowel higher)

CELL BLOCKS

			4	
5			4	4
3	2			
		1		2
			5	
3			3	

WORKOUT 162

SUDOKU

3	2	1	4
1	4	3	2
2	1	4	3
4	3	2	1

4	1	2	3
2	3	4	1
1	2	3	4
3	4	1	2

4	3	2	1
2	1	3	4
3	4	1	2
1	2	4	3

ADD UP
1 30
2 33
3 46

WORKOUT 163

CODEWORDS

SPOT THE SUM
1 23 (9+14) **2** 20 (4+16)
3 18 (4+14) **4** 32 (13+19)

SOLUTIONS

WORKOUT 164
PIECEWORD

F	O	L	K		U	S	E	R
O		E		A		C		E
A	D	V	A	N	T	A	G	E
M		I		T		N		L
	E	V	I	C	T			
L	I	D	O		H	Y	M	N
M		L		E		A		
T	A	L	C		R	U	N	G
G		A		V		I		
V	E	I	N		I	T	C	H
	N	O	B	L	E			
I		V		R		M		T
B	E	E	K	E	E	P	E	R
I		R		W		L		A
S	I	T	E		L	E	V	Y

WORKOUT 165
FUTOSHIKI

2	3	1
1	2	3
3	1	2

SPLITS
1 Meringues **2** Historian
3 Rigmarole **4** Leniently
5 Patriarch

DISAVOWEL

O	R	A	L		J		P	O	O	L
R	E	C	I	T	A	L		R	U	E
G	A	T	E	A	U		C	A	R	S
A	D	O		U	N	C	U	T		I
N		R	A	N	D		P	O	L	O
	B		S	T	I	R		R	U	N
R	O	M	P		C	O	N		P	
H	O	E		M	E	L	O	D	I	C
I	N	D	I	A		L	I	A	N	A
N		I		G	U	E	S	T		L
O	K	A	P	I		R	E	A	L	M

WORKOUT 166
FITWORD

G	U	L	L	I	B	L	E
A		S		I		A		I
C	H	E	C	K		T	U	G
I			E	A	T		H
D	A	T	E	D		L	O	T
	O			E		
C	U	R		V	I	R	U	S
H		R	O	E			O
I	R	E		N	E	W	L	Y
N		N		O		A		A
O	P	T	I	M	I	S	T

Zest

SHAPE UP

D	T	M	D	B	W	H	C	B	W
E	A	A	V	A	A	A	H	R	E
L	L	H	O	R	G	N	O	A	B
I	L	L	R	T	N	D	P	H	E
U	I	E	A	O	E	E	I	M	R
S	S	R	K	K	R	L	N	S	N

WORKOUT 167
PATHFINDER

T	Y	A	H	S	E	D	O	T	R	E
R	D	T	S	A	L	D	E	E	P	D
E	N	I	P	I	N	K	R	C	M	N
K	U	O	T	L	H	S	L	E	E	A
B	O	E	P	S	U	F	F	Y	R	A
R	E	P	M	S	E	C	N	E	B	M
A	M	L	I	T	E	F	U	S	L	E
U	B	P	O	R	K	L	O	O	M	S
L	O	M	L	H	I	W	H	C	R	T
A	T	S	L	K	L	A	E	M	A	R
T	E	S	C	U	T	T	L	E	D	I

MOSEY, RAMBLE, STRIDE,
MARCH, WALK, HIKE,
FLOUNCE, STROLL, STOMP,
LIMP, SLINK, SHUFFLE, CREEP,
MEANDER, TODDLE, SASHAY,
TREK, BOUND, TIPTOE,
PERAMBULATE, SCUTTLE

SPOT THE SUM
1 23 (7+16) **2** 27 (4+23)

OPPOSITES ATTRACT
1 Follow/lead **2** Double/half
3 Active/passive **4** Extend/
retract **5** Obedient/rebellious

WORKOUT 168
DOMINOES
1 Pamela **2** Graeme **3** Goldie
4 Arnold **5** Stuart **6** Petula

SUDOKU

6	8	7	1	4	9	2	3	5
3	9	5	8	6	2	4	1	7
1	4	2	3	5	7	8	6	9
9	1	8	6	2	4	5	7	3
7	3	6	5	8	1	9	2	4
2	5	4	7	9	3	1	8	6
5	6	9	2	7	8	3	4	1
8	7	3	4	1	5	6	9	2
4	2	1	9	3	6	7	5	8

CODEWORDS
1 Dock **2** Crew **3** Keel **4** Hold
5 Rudder (9=W, 10=L, 11=H,
12=U)

WORKOUT 169
NUMBER JIG
1 298 **2** 635 **3** 6402 **4** 5034

WORDSEARCH

LETTER SEQUENCE
1 J (alternate +5, -3) **2** D (-2,
-3, -4…) **3** S (+2, -4, +6, -8…)
4 S (initial letters of numbers
– well done if you got this)
5 M (+2, +1, +3, +2…)

WORKOUT 170
WILD WORDS
1 Age before beauty **2** North
Star **3** On the up **4** Full house

SMART SUMS
1 56 (60-4) **2** 20 (14+6) **3** 24
(3x8) **4** 5 (10÷2) **5** 36 (6x6)

KAKURO

	5	9	7	8		9	7
5	7	8	9	6	3	1	4	2
8	9			9	6	3	8

WORKOUT 171
ARROWORD

	U		A		R			D
S	I	D	E	I	S	S	U	E
E		S		P	A	P		T
A	D	D		P	R	O	S	E
C	A	P		L	A	N	E	S
A	R	O	S	E		G	E	T
R	E	P		S	L	E	D	S

SMALL CHANGE
1 Drill, Hammer, Wrench, Saw, Plane **2** Ravel, Bach, Bizet, Handel, Brahms **3** Shatter, Smash, Break, Snap, Crack **4** Stage, Curtain, Play, Cast, Gods

FUTOSHIKI

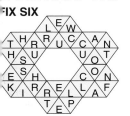

WORKOUT 172
FIX SIX

(hexagon word puzzle: T H R U C A N, H S U U O T, E S H C O N, K I R E L L A F, T P E)

MOBILE CODE
1 Tie **2** String **3** Ribbon **4** Cotton **5** Stomach

FOUR BY FOUR

C	O	R	K
A	M	E	N
P	I	L	E
S	T	Y	E

WORKOUT 173
SPOT THE SUM
1 18 (5+13) **2** 29 (13+16)

SPLITS
1 Bobsleigh **2** Newsagent **3** Grievance **4** Doughnuts **5** Neutrally

TAKE FIVE

M	U	F	T	I
U		A		N
F	A	T	A	L
T		A		E
I	N	L	E	T

WORKOUT 174
MINI JIGSAW
Medway, Severn, Thames, Liffey, Jordan, Humber

KILLER SUDOKU

3	8	2	9	7	1	6	5	4
9	7	5	3	4	6	1	8	2
6	4	1	8	2	5	7	9	3
5	1	4	6	8	9	2	3	7
2	6	8	4	3	7	9	1	5
7	9	3	1	5	2	8	4	6
8	3	9	2	6	4	5	7	1
1	5	6	7	9	3	4	2	8
4	2	7	5	1	8	3	6	9

WORKOUT 175
LOGICAL
Barry, Dracula, 3rd
Harry, Tarzan, 1st
Larry, Superman, 2nd

STAIRCASE
Film set, costume, biopic, X-rated, bit part, montage, outtake.

The "staircase" reveals:
FOOTAGE

WORD BUILDER
Amber, Brace, Break, Bench, Baker, Rehab, Backer, Banker, Branch, Embark, Camber, Breach, Chamber, Bracken, Benchmark

WORKOUT 176
OPPOSITES ATTRACT
1 LIGHT and DARK
2 BEFORE and AFTER
3 PROUD and ASHAMED
4 COARSE and REFINED

SET SQUARE

7	+	8	−	6
+				x
9	−	2	+	1
÷		÷		÷
4	+	5	÷	3

IN AND OUT
Tramp (+ M), scut (- O), roué (+ U), moor (- T), bathed (+ H)
MOUTH

Put (- O), gape (- R), tier (- G), wheat (+ A), brine (+ N)
ORGAN

WORKOUT 177
WORDSEARCH

W	S	K	X	M	O	H
I	Y	T	B	A	A	K
N	Z	W	U	N	I	R
D	H	F	O	A	U	O
S	P	V	N	R	Y	O
O	E	R	O	D	U	T
R	D	T	C	L	G	Q

C	T	L	C	N	D	W
R	X	O	I	H	E	F
J	U	S	T	I	S	Y
V	A	S	C	A	E	M
B	Q	N	R	G	R	K
P	K	R	A	P	T	E
T	L	E	B	D	B	Z

THREE IN ONE
1 Port **2** Bolt **3** Watch **4** Banger **5** Match

CELL BLOCKS

(grid puzzle with values: 5, 2, 3, 3, 2, 2, 3, 6, 4, 6)

221

SOLUTIONS

WORKOUT 178
SUDOKU

4	1	3	2
3	2	1	4
2	3	4	1
1	4	2	3

2	4	3	1
3	1	2	4
1	3	4	2
4	2	1	3

4	1	2	3
2	3	4	1
1	2	3	4
3	4	1	2

ADD UP
1 30
2 47
3 52

WORKOUT 179
NUMBER MAZE

18	10	21	66	33	96	94	54	34	36	25	12
66	97	44	90	92	18	32	42	13	26	39	68
78	34	73	42	62	24	99	36	66	78	96	66
30	24	15	18	42	30	56	68	74	86	88	18
19	36	22	36	24	66	72	96	6	27	91	24
25	54	84	18	26	72	54	84	36	67	78	6
55	24	56	52	62	68	75	74	25	92	84	26
22	60	32	18	30	42	78	24	11	82	90	11
18	30	28	24	20	88	86	48	54	42	60	33
14	40	38	96	40	22	14	34	38	10	28	80
86	96	30	42	62	22	22	22	22	22	22	22
19	18	35	23	92	22	22	22	22	22	22	22

SO COMPLETE

Idle	Lend	Bard	D
Torn	Polo	Over	O
Laze	Zeal	Jazz	Z
Bear	Chew	Here	E
Town	Scan	Acne	N

WORKOUT 180
NUMBER JIG

4	■	2	8	3	2	1	■	9
5	5	6	3	■	5	4	3	8
3	4	4	3	■	4	5	4	2
8	3	9	■	3	3	2	5	7
■	2	■	2	8	7	■	6	■
3	3	1	5	7	■	3	5	9
6	4	3	4	■	6	4	4	8
4	5	1	2	■	3	4	3	4
9	■	2	8	2	3	1	■	2

Leftover number: **2518**

WORKOUT 181
SCRAMBLE
1 Owl **2** Goose **3** Penguin
4 Falcon **5** Starling
6 Pheasant **7** Albatross
8 Woodpecker

INITIALS
1. Statue of Liberty
2. Lily-of-the-Valley
3. *The Merchant of Venice*
4. *Paint It Black*
5. King Charles Spaniel

HONEYCOMB
1 Before **2** Coffee **3** Scrawl
4 Bellow **5** Search
6 Camera **7** Narrow
8 Catnap **9** Negate
10&11 Free of charge

WORKOUT 182
FITWORD

S	P	L	I	C	I	N	G
E		L		N	N		A
V	I	A		T	A	K	E	N
I		T		E			G
C	H	E	E	R	I	N	G
T		A		A		E		N
	B	U	T	C	H	E	R	Y
S			T		D		M
M	U	F	T	I		I	M	P
U		L		N		E		H
T	H	U	G	G	E	R	Y

Narrator

MINI JIGSAW
Bronte, Greene, Huxley
Alcott, Orwell, Conrad

WORKOUT 183
PATHFINDER

N	I	A	T	N	U	O	M	H
A	C	C	U	A	S	D	G	C
G	H	B	A	L	E	I	H	D
G	U	L	O	B	E	A	C	R
O	T	P	C	L	I	S	U	A
B	E	E	S	R	E	N	R	O
O	S	B	L	T	F	I	L	B
T	O	I	A	A	X	W	I	W
B	F	K	J	Q	H	O	N	O
T	S	L	U	G	E	C	G	N
A	P	R	E	S	S	K	I	S

NUMBER JIG
1 737 **2** 157 **3** 3949

PAIRS
Boiled egg, boyfriend, courtesy light, custard apple, grand piano, hard cheese, master switch, night school, opera glasses, power station, Sunday best, title fight

MOSS and PLATES yield EPSOM SALTS

WORKOUT 184
MANOR BORN
Photo 1

SUDOKU

7	4	6	2	3	1	5	9	8
2	9	5	4	7	8	1	6	3
1	8	3	9	6	5	7	2	4
8	2	9	5	1	3	6	4	7
6	3	7	8	4	2	9	1	5
4	5	1	7	9	6	3	8	2
9	1	8	3	5	4	2	7	6
5	7	2	6	8	9	4	3	1
3	6	4	1	2	7	8	5	9

SPLITS
1 Automatic **2** Secretary
3 Nocturnal **4** Vegetable
5 Quarterly

SOLUTIONS

WORKOUT 185

WORD BUILDER
Litre, Alert, Tiler, Delta, Later, Ideal, Retail, Mailed, Mallet, Redial, Detail, Miller, Literal, Trailed, Tallied, Trialled, Treadmill

WORD SEARCH

CODEWORDS
1 Sea 2 Crab 3 Coast (9=T) 4 Resort 5 Bathers

WORKOUT 186

SMALL CHANGE
1 Dirk, Dagger, Spear, Mace, Club 2 Big, Large, Grand, Vast, Huge 3 Mango, Next, Oasis, Burton, Gap 4 Spire, Nave, Altar, Crypt, Pew

KAKURO

3	1			2	3	1	5
8	6	7	9	4	1	2	3	5
2	4	7	1			1	2

WORKOUT 187

ARROWORD

SCRAMBLE
1 Bar 2 Inn 3 Café 4 Bistro 5 Eatery 6 Taverna 7 Hostelry 8 Brasserie

INITIALS
1. *One Foot in the Grave*
2. Wolfgang Amadeus Mozart
3. Hide-and-Seek
4. *You Only Live Twice*
5. A stitch in time saves nine

WORKOUT 188

MINI FIT
1 Tor 2 Den 3 Weak 4 Swat

VOWEL PLAY
1 Violin 2 Trumpet 3 Guitar 4 Accordion 5 Piano 6 Oboe 7 Bassoon 8 Flute 9 Organ 10 Cello

SET SQUARE

4	+	7	−	8
+		−		−
9	+	1	÷	5
−		×		×
2	+	3	+	6

WORKOUT 189

SPOT THE SUM
1 24 (8+16) 2 26 (4+22) 3 22 (9+13) 4 33 (12+21)

BOX WISE
1 Con 2 Sha 3 Man 4 Tra 5 Sup 6 Per 7 Cer 8 Ise 9 Mit 10 Res 11 Eal 12 Ult

STAIRCASE
Taggart, Hi-De-Hi!, Spender, Mr Bean, Frasier, Angels, Pop Idol.

The "staircase" reveals: **THE BILL**

WORKOUT 190

MINI JIGSAW
Mirror, Clutch, Englne Hubcap, Bonnet, Towbar

SIX PACK

			7	2		
		1	3		4	6
	3	7	8	1	9	4
1	2	4	2	3	2	3	9
3	8	1	5	6	1	6	4
6	5	6	7	4	9	2	1
	3	2	1	2	3	4
		4	5	6	1	
			7	4		